This Shit Crazy

Tre Prince

Cadmus Publishing
www.cadmuspublishing.com

Copyright © 2022 Tre Prince

Cover art by Tre Prince

Published by Cadmus Publishing
www.cadmuspublishing.com
Port Angeles, WA

ISBN: 987-1-63751-196-1
Library of Congress Control Number: 2022908688

All rights reserved. Copyright under Berne Copyright Convention, Universal Copyright Convention, and Pan-American Copyright Convention. No part of this book may be reproduced, stored in a retrieval system, or transmitted in any form, or by any means, electronic, mechanical, photocopying, recording or otherwise, without prior permission of the author.

Dedication

To my Godfather and big homey Lil Loco, thanks for acknowledging my growth and assisting my endeavors. To Ricky 'Freeway' Ross, I appreciate the guidance, accepting my calls, and your assistance. I'd like to also dedicate this to all the names I mentioned in this book because you all helped color the truth and the message I've given. And to my mother and father, for you were both divinely chosen to be my entry into this world. And last, I would like to shout out Linden K. Millar—I told you I would.

Synopsis:

This Shit Crazy is a look into society from the intellectual viewpoint of a divine spirit that is incarcerated physically but not mentally, inside an imprisoned society of the mind.

This here is a memoir of humor, truth, and personal events that gives color to life, tragedy, and politics that shape American society through sports, music, fashion, incarceration and epidemic.

Follow this great message and find from it a greater *you* within you, by Divine intervention.

Forethought:

May whoever picks this book up not only enjoy it but also find the center of your existence within yourself, to grow and experience life therefrom. There is massive power dormant within you that awaits your use of it. Those that already know this, know I have your best interest at heart.

Hotep.

Tre Prince ~ THA L'OK

"I am the Master of my fate

I am the Captain of my Soul."—The Prosperity Bible

Table of Contents

Introduction 1

Kobe Bryant / LA 15

Every Day I'm Hustling 23

Sports & Culture 29

I Felt it for Real 39

Creativity 45

Passion 47

South Central, The Angels 51

A Man Falls, His Legacy Rises 56

Motivation 59

Closer 62

Introduction

On this day, April 21, 2020, I finally awaken from sleep at the crack of dawn. But only after a restless night of tossing and turning, waking up twice to piss, before lying back down and dozing off; I wake back up to make wudu, then prayer, before again lying back in bed but only to meditate on my prayers; I finally fall asleep but wake up again thirty minutes later. And so I say to myself, "This Shit Crazy."

However, this expression is not made because of a restless night of sleep. And I am very much thankful to the Creator to have awoken, fallen asleep, and awoken again. But today is not about another day of living per se. Instead, more so than less, I wake up this morning with my mind keen, and feeling thankful for my awareness, to be able to differentiate reality and my own thoughts from the illusion that has befallen, and presently is befalling, society. Yes. And so, more importantly, I am thankful for the patience, strength, and tolerance to endure and overcome all the bullshit—the fear, doubt, and anxiety—that comes as pressure, obstacles, or hardship placed on my soul (mind) that is still seeking joy and freedom during this mundane experience called life. What experience(s) specifically? I'm getting there.

I roll out of bed and stand directly inside a partial bathroom, which I am fucked up about living in. Even more so because I have to share this intimate space with another male, who is lying in a separate bunk right over my shoulder still asleep, or pretending to be. Whatever. How come I must share this intimate space? Because I am incarcerated, and certain essential human rights at the moment I am not privileged to receive as a prisoner. For a prime example, privacy.

And so, I seriously question: what differentiates being human, by right or act of civility and of being a civilized living being, which is essential to all living beings, from that which is inhuman, by action or definition?

Or, how can you separate what is thought and deemed a civil right, from a natural human right, conscientiously, without a person being inhumane to another living being? Regardless of what you penalize a person for, or consider them as being?

I take a look at a place like Sweden, where you hardly hear anything about crime, or surely not anything bad for the most part. And I acknowledge the way it reforms prison inmates and the model structure of its prisons, which are equivalent to three- and four-star hotels here in America. Now this only registers to me mostly because of my current circumstances; however, the way Sweden still treats her convicted, imprisoned, or unruly citizens as civilized human beings, regardless of what she has penalized a person for or considers them as, is humane. This can only make a person, criminals included, want to be a part of a truly humane and civilized society. And so, therefore, act responsibly.

But then again, who am I looking to make sense to other than myself... "This Shit Crazy!"

It is whispered or said, but low enough not to wake anyone up, that "The captor over a period of time creates their captive(s). But as a result, and over the course of time and occurrences, the captive(s) becomes a reflection of their captor. That being said, it is only wise that the captive know that they can learn a lot about their captor by studying themselves. Then through this method discover the means to obtain freedom from the captor's illusion effect." Makes sense to me. Wake up! You are not oppressed. It is but a thought.

I buss down and do five hundred push-ups, then the same total of squats, fifty a set, for a count of ten sets. My mind is ticking and tocking like a clock, with thoughts and images that are of my own will—but also those that are not, unfortunately. Meaning a thought not my own, that is instead a distraction to me, like someone else's thoughts spoken out loud or traveling through a Universal Mind invisibly, at the frequency to which I'm channeled. I wish I could better pause the part of the mind's faculty that controls thought and thinking, then resume it only when I'm ready for conscious thought. Or quickly learn how to channel my frequency of thoughts; because the bombardment of unwanted thoughts is overwhelming at times. It is a task I'm training to fulfil.

After the mid to light workout, I wash up before breakfast, standing inside the same cell but with a sheet hung up from a clothing line, and washing inside the single sink of the cell. The same sink I use to wash my face, brush my teeth, and drink water from. Perfectly abnormal, right? Anyhow, I wash up while I wear a face mask. I also wore this mask while I slept during the night as an extra precaution. Strangely, though, I sense that the picture that has been painted of there being a pandemic in the world from a virus outbreak, referred to as COVID-19, is more propaganda at this point—now over two months into it—than it is a factual health crisis that is killing 'some people.' Not all.

Nevertheless, I will continue to herd along with the masses, until I eventually, individually, feel certain that I am safe to breathe without catching this labeled-respirator disease, which has been claimed to be derived from a region of the world that currently carries a stigma--for assassinating using chemical gases that attack the respiratory system, collapsing the lungs and causing cardiac arrest, then immediate death. What COVID-19 is also supposed to do. Still, the crazy part in all this is—in the midst of the country's lockdowns in the majority of states, many are losing their livelihood, businesses, homes, opportunities, and so on. All while also losing their lives or watching their loved ones perish. The outcome: frustration, anger, depression, anxiety, hate and racism towards our Asian brothas and sistas; fear, and *debt*.

Frustration, anger, depression, and anxiety are all understandable; the world is in a crisis. Racism and hatred, is ignorance, the common Western-American's behavior. And fear is a predictable result: a no brainer. But now, debt? Having to owe or forfeit while at the same time being restricted from your normal means or a means period to pay; this I have a problem with.

Ain't no way that an allegedly great country should put its working class, law abiding, and/or retired citizens under the duress of debt or grappling to repay loans, take in earnings, or beg for money in many cases, during a health crisis that causes them to stay at home and essentially not earn a wage. I think, or would have done if the power was mine to do so, it would be better to exempt people from all bills and expenses relative to emergency travel and the means to (car, monthly insurance), shelter—primary residence (monthly rent, mortgage, land taxes)—and healthcare emergencies at the bare minimum (including health insurance). Or I would simply discontinue such expenses until after I was certain the country was safe enough for people to resume fending for themselves. Not failing to mention I would have to provide food for all in desperate need of it. It would only be fair. Right?

No one should lose or sacrifice more than the pandemic has already taken by demise, with their demise. But then again, who am I to anyone other than myself, family, and close peers? Oh yeah, that's right. I'm someone a jury convicted for one count of conspiracy to commit Hobbs Act Robbery; count two, Hobbs Act Robbery; and count three, 924(c) discharge of a firearm causing death. ?

Though I will say this: my compassion for the lives of innocent people is greater than that of the government's agents and prosecutors, who obtained a wrongful conviction against me by committing prosecutorial misconduct, tampering with physical evidence, and using tainted hearsay testimony, defrauding me of my innocence and right to a fair trial.

But that's a later story. Back to the point I'm making, from a capitalist-driven society point of view. Leaders today will say that the pandemic crisis was good for change, period, right? But of course it will not be relayed in that manner. Instead the words used will be how we all persevered, how we overcame, or how we battled through the pandemic as a nation that brought about change. Yeah, but at whose cost? Know your captor. This Shit Crazy!

As I pen this, whatever you want to call it: book, partial biography, work, or art piece, I must say I would have never have thought I'd be writing non-fiction about an historical event or people that have impacted my life. In fact, to add truth to the tale, I never imagined being a writer until after I came into my adulthood. While growing up, and as early as the age of five, I only imagined being an artist. I had a stepfather named Smiley, a.k.a. Six Dollars, an Original godfather then a Harlem Crip, who introduced me first to art. And he encouraged my artistry too by aiding me with my own paint brushes, pencils, paint color kit and an easel and paper. I would paint horses, cowboys, houses, and the sun. This was when I was four and five years of age.

But by the age of seven I had a new interest; now I was intrigued with being a musician, which is still an interest of mine today. Back then, however, I could write my own lyrics and perform them by age nine. The young act at the time, Kris Kross, didn't have nothing on me. Wasn't even competition. Just kidding. But even so, that was predominantly how it was when it came to a dream or act of interest as a kid, and even as a teen. So to be writing, and at the level that I am, for me is an unforeseen revelation in my personal calling.

I was born in the early 1980s, and raised in South Central Los Angeles, California. Prior to having any understanding of life or living, I found my life had been subjected to the statistic that one out of every three to five black males born in the inner city ghettos of America will be dead or imprisoned by age twenty-five. And also probably will succumb to unemployment, a lack of education or higher learning, and be insufficient men, absent fathers to children, drug addicts, alcoholics, and criminals. I surely fell victim to this preconditioned generational crisis, which should have been identified and labeled as such by the President, Congress, the Senate, the State Attorney General, the United Nations—a pandemic in its own right: a social, economic, and racial demise. But again, who am I looking to make sense to other than myself, or possibly you? This Shit Crazy!

Besides, it doesn't change the outcome that was predicted nearly forty years ago. Nor what I and many others, both still alive or now dead, have experienced already. On second thought, I can honestly say now that I've taken the bad predicament I was put into, and set up to fail, and done myself justice by it. Because moving forward I will never again go through what I have already been through.

Again, what I and others have gone through, for better or worse—I hope this can possibly change the circumstances and outcome for the younger generations living today, or who are yet unborn, but who will be born into the same or similar preconditioned crisis: a social, economic, and racial demise.

And I use the phrase 'racial demise' because it is destructive for a soul and spirit to be born into this world and later tainted with racism in any form—racial prejudices or hatred Not only do I see this effect in others but, sadly, I see it also in myself. And I feel that my innocence has been robbed in that regard. Right? This Shit Crazy!

Breakfast arrives at the door of the cell, something like room service. It's really not, although some may call it so in here. However, the meal is passed through a tray slot, and you still have to get up and get it.

Today's morning meal is some generic brand flakes cereal, skim milk, and a dry-ass piece of cake that is freezer bit cold. Still and truly, I crush it! Nine minutes tops. Then slide the empty tray, bashing it into the door for pickup. "Come and get this shit!" I say aloud to myself; then chuckle a small laugh. It's a prison antic.

Anyway, I was hungry for why I ate this meal; after describing it as a hospital ward dish. But then, I naturally love cereal with milk, and I can eat almost any kind of cereal—though those brand flakes I just finished chowing I am not a fan of. And the frozen thaw cake was trash. However, I am thankful to not be hungry or have to go without a meal. So don't get it twisted; I'm not complaining. Just calling it as it is.

Well I hope in God that today brings good news: no matter if it only be something good happening elsewhere in the world. Because regardless of the pandemic there is always good going on in the world—God-Allah-Jehovah-Buddha-Ausar—The Creator is the pure essence of good. And don't nothing else come from it but perfection in good. Therefore, I hope that I'm open enough to receive good today, like favorable news in my appeal.

I follow current case law rulings that come down from the Supreme, Circuit, and district courts of law, how the twelve disciples followed Jesus (Yehoshua) seeking to learn law and receive their blessings from God (Yahweh). In due prayer I will be rewarded by the Almighty Creator. This I am faithful in knowing.

In fact, as I sit and lean back onto the bed, I'm reminded how close to receiving my blessing I am. Or better, the realization that I am blessed; that the blessing I seek I have already received. Believing is knowing—seeing or receiving is the effect. Correct?

Covering the space of a plain wall above the foot of the top bunk I sleep in is two court cases that each have favorable rulings that I printed out and taped there to serve for a vision board: US v. Ray Chea, 2019 US District LEXIS 77651—ruling that a Hobbs Act Robbery is not categorically a crime of violence under the elements clause of the Statute 924(c), because the Statute can be committed by causing fear of future injury to property. And next, US v. Randy Irvin Begay, 2019 US App. LEXIS 24608, ruling in the Ninth Circuit Court of Appeals that second degree murder can be committed recklessly and therefore does not categorically constitute a "crime of violence" under the elements clause of Statute 18 USC 924(c)(3)(A). This establishes the degree of "intent" in "physical force" now doctrined by law for the purpose of defining the same identical language in Statute 18 USC 16's "Crime of Violence" clause, which indisputably requires intentional conduct. Meaning, purposeful; previously established in Johnson v. US, 559 US 133(2010) interpreting the requirement of force be used "against' someone or something, suggests that "violent force" require "a higher degree of intent than negligent or merely accidental conduct."

The reason for why these cases and the laws are of great magnitude to me is because at this point, ten years after being convicted, and sixteen years since my arrest, I have to challenge my convictions at an angle other than just attacking the guilty verdict against me to prevail and see the light of day. The odds, politically, are never in a defendant's favor. Especially post-conviction. So to see relief, or have a favorable angle to exploit, I must take it to make it home. I can reestablish my innocence another way, or at a later date. That's not the door that is open for me at the moment. The door that is open, cracked and widening, is within the "crime of violence" clause being newly interpreted and applied today to various charges. By which the statute enhances federal sentences, specifically mine.

Due to the sentence enhancement penalty for crimes considered violent, there is now a great percentage of convicted persons in prison and crowding the system, who are serving sentences of over twenty years to life. But take away the enhancement, and almost every sentence being served by a defendant convicted of a violent felony in federal court (and state) by statute of the charged controlling case, does not exceed twenty to twenty-five years; the maximum punishment allowed, other than a monetary fine, for the majority of crimes being criminally prosecuted.

And so when you take that away, it helps reduce taxes by reducing the overcrowding in the prison system, starting with thousands of prisoners that have been incarcerated past the maximum sentence allowed by statute, minus the enhancement(s).

I hear and read a lot about prison reform, unjust sentencing, or sentence reductions being law. Well, if you erase sentence enhancements, and couple that with prison rehabilitation and post-release treatment, rather than the current system of correctional prisons and post release probation or parole, the result will likely be prison reform and a start to a better free society.

Remember, we can always take a look at a place like Sweden for guidance. Or, for debate, places like China or Korea, which have a no-tolerance view on crime and prison systems that aren't a thriving business. America at times appears to be making reform but for some reason never completely make the transition. Why? "Know the Captor." This Shit Crazy!

Two years ago and during a discussion on the topic of politics in America, I told several fellow convicts that with President Donald J. Trump in office (the Republican Party) I'm going home; I'm being released from incarceration. And no, I am not a Trump supporter, per se (nor am I against him); or a supporter of any president or American political branch of government. I don't choose a side in any of that. I'm quite indifferent to be exact. I only care to know how a party's actions particularly suit my needs. Or which may possibly be detrimental to my well-being and freedom. Plus, when you stand outside the box, you have all the room to wiggle.

Anyhow, the reason I made my statement about being released while Trump is in office was because, for one, I saw that the door was cracked for my opportunity. But just as I observed the door being cracked, I also got the impression that the president and Republican Party have to free his pirates and cronies, or those closely related to pirates and cronies, associated with his voters and presidential campaign supporters. And so I plan to catch the wave that's heading to the shores of freedom. And wealth. You see, what I have come to understand about politics but which once went over my head is that politics in itself is of no magnitude. Instead, it is the politicians that are the cosmic forces behind the result of politics. And also, those affected by politics (you and I), are the ones who help put politicians in a place to make a significant change in your life or agenda; these are the two cosmic forces of politics. This is why I say, "Know the Captor." I clearly don't know Trump, but I can see and study the characteristics of such a person and personally judge how I can or cannot benefit from him. Besides, it is all an illusion anyhow. I am the only one who truly has the power to make change over me. "Understand the captive effect."

Lastly, I'll add this: "There is no Western Power in the history of its ruling that the underworld isn't the parent or child to." So whenever an elected official or heir to the throne takes position in office, so does the underworld. Now this doesn't necessarily mean that the underworld is [entirely] an evil entity. But face it, the entire modern world is corrupted. However, look at it this way—and why I say that I'm going to catch that wave headed to freedom shores from prison. A prison I shouldn't be in to begin with.

Let's say you took office as heir to the throne; and let's say you had a child, sibling, parent, relative or friend, or were intimately close to someone else that did, and the significant person was in prison. And anywhere from a day to thirty years has been served on their sentence; you would naturally have some compassion or obligation to set that person free if you had the power to and believed that it was for good cause. Correct? Or at least the common person would feel obligated to, or feel compassion to do so, which brings me to a point.

The President of the United States of America has the chief executive power to pardon Charles Manson from prison if he chose to. And has the executive power to appoint an attorney to serve as Attorney General or as a Supreme Court Justice. These are two significant executive acts of judicial legislative power essential to law and freedom.

Since President Donald J. Trump has been in office he has so far pardoned several of his cronies or of those closely associated to him (as do the majority of presidents) and has appointed two Justices to the bench. His appointed Justices have each made pivotal rulings in cases that now provide me with a means to either vacate or reverse the convictions held against me. In fact, favorable court rulings in: Sessions v. Dimaya, and United States v. Davis, have each, respectively, set the wheels in motion for letting parties of the underworld, or those closely related to it, free from prison. Like in the US v. Johnson case I mentioned earlier, which gave life to these cases now. So the wheels have now been rolling for ten years.

Although I have no lineage or other ties to powerful underworld leaders, the criminal charges against me nevertheless fall under the criminal statute that was intended to bring order to the undisciplined heirs of the monarch. This is one way I plan to catch that wave I keep mentioning headed to shore. Again, my initial way is actual innocence. But politically I fit the profile of guilt; so damn innocence in some respects. I've been crying and showing my wrongful convictions to the wrong judicial system now for sixteen years. I'm forced to explore other means for relief. 'Know your Captor!' I do.

The charge of the Hobbs Act, like RICCO and the Continued Criminal Enterprise (CCE) statutes were not intended by Congress, when first written, to target inner city local crimes committed by local hoodlums or low-level criminals. No. These are statues that were designed to prevent large corporations and mafia enterprises (the underworld) from committing economic international or interstate private and commercial infractions of law (crimes) without penalty. However, that all began to change roughly thirty to forty years ago. An opportunity was presented to capitalist politicians to create and seize a billion dollars annually from the prison industry. The revenue would come from taxpayer dollars for the filling up of over thirty federal prisons, and another significant amount in state and private-run prisons, all built within the same time span of the last thirty to forty years. It isn't a coincidence, accident, or secret that mass incarceration is big and has been big in America now for forty years or more. Or that minorities or low-level criminals are serving as commodity stock.

But that is another story to tell. Just understand your captor or its captivity effect. And know that whenever a new prison is built, especially if none are being closed down, then somebody (you or I) is projected to fill its vacancy. Also, you don't have to be a crook or bad person to be detained or sent to prison. Marcus Garvey wasn't a crook or bad person; neither were Rosa Parks, Martin Luther King Jr., Nelson Mandela, Gandhi, and many others who were detained for whatever reason. Today it is about you being a commodity. As it was before slavery was outlawed here in America. This Shit Crazy!

As I kick back on the bed and stare at my vision board, long after breakfast has been served, and now lunch about an hour ago, there is also a color photo print-out taped there of the cover design of my first published novel a couple months ago: *Bounce Back Joe*. An achievement I consider great, because I was able to accomplish something that is morally considered great, but while in a dysfunctional, imprisoned, physical environment. For many here they are not only physically imprisoned but also mentally so. Which makes the mind and body dysfunctional, creating the same atmosphere. And so for anyone incarcerated to be able to let their mind and imagination go free and create something that people in society can enjoy, value, and ultimately appreciate you for, is a great achievement. By my definition at least.

I first started novel writing in the summer of 2005 while in SHU lockup. It began as a means to vent, or for me to wander away. Like I find with songwriting. But by the time the first chapter was complete I had seen how I could add to my legacy in life. Now I wasn't then, nor am I today, a world renowned figure. But I am widely known amongst my family, friends, and prior foes who are now loved ones. Which is all smooth with me. However, and what also inspired this creative spark in me, were the national and international figures of my generation, that had sprung up or were springing up in music, films, TV, theater, sports, fashion, journalism, politics, and on Wall Street. Many derive from the inner cities (the streets) and family backgrounds similar to my own. Or worse. So heck, I felt like I could still make it in becoming somebody great that contributed to society; fuck what the government's federal prosecutors were prosecuting me for. As long as I was alive and my mind free, I had action. That was my attitude then, and it still is today. Because, as my beloved homeboy William Vashawn Fields a.k.a. Baby Trey Devil recently quoted to me in a letter, in regard to me publishing my first book under these circumstances I mention before, "We are only limited to the restrictions we place on ourselves in the end." That is a fact.

Legends like Kobe Bryant, Nipsy Hussle, and COVID-19 victims Ellis Marsalis (jazz pianist and jazz musician educator) and Sergio Rossi (Italian shoe designer) have all impacted my life either intellectually or spiritually. Though Kobe and Nipsy I feel the more emotionally connected to, and so I am the most affected by, off-hand. Mainly because of the closeness in our generation. Upon the news of each of their deaths within a year apart, it felt like I had lost someone I personally knew. And I hadn't formally met either of them. Still, the pain was real. Here's why…

The Prince

Part 1
Legacy

Chapter 1

Kobe Bryant / LA

The year was 2002, as I recall. The Los Angeles Lakers were balling and in the second round of the NBA Playoffs against the San Antonio Spurs. It was looking like they could advance all the way to the finals and contend for a third consecutive year to win a Chip, with Shaq and Kobe on the roster. But, also, they boasted a well-equipped supporting cast: Derrick Fisher at point guard, Rick Fox at small forward, and a natural six-man off the bench straight stud, Robert Horry at power forward. Plus a respected bench that was deep. But the key to it all was Coach Phil Jackson. Yes, it was certainly possible that they could win back to back to back titles. In fact, it was not easy for any sports analyst or fan of basketball to realistically dispute otherwise, but for argument's sake. The year before, they had swept one of the greatest guards to play the game at his position in his era, Allen Iverson, and the 76ers. And the year before that they'd beat Reggie Miller, a straight shooter from anywhere on the court, plus Jalen Rose and the Indiana Pacers. Both these teams in the finals. Not to mention overcoming adversity for the Lakers to get to the Finals. With having to battle teams like Chris Webber and the Sacramento Kings that took them to a hard fought game 7. The purple and gold were hot. The home team had the city cracc'n. I'd never witnessed anything like it, personally, as a fan of any sport, the impact that the LA Lakers had on the culture of Los Angeles, California as a championship pedigree team. Back when Magic Johnson, Kareem, A.J. Green, Byron Scott and others I can't recall at the moment were on the rosters, with Pat Riley as head coach, had the city bleed purple and gold, I was a young boy. And so I didn't know a damn thing about a city or state standing behind its home team in national sports the way I witnessed and understood it later. I had been too young at the time to truly appreciate the experience of Bo Jackson and the LA Raiders having the city on lock. But now I know why Ice Cube always kept a LA Raiders hat on over his curl. But then, too, the LA Kings starring Wayne Gretzky had the city poppin' back in the day. Seeing and understanding now what a sports team means to a society of people, the LA Lakers was and is a fan tradition for many. Like how religion is to the worshiper, or Kwanzaa is to the celebrator...

I had been home a little under five months early in the year of '02, after maxing out a three-year CYA sentence on an eight-month violation, stemming from a simple gun possession charge I caught as a juvenile in 1998; almost two years after Kobe came into the league and bagged my celebrity-crush girlfriend, Brandy. I thought he would keep her and go on to marry her. But I guessed wrong. His own crush girlfriend, Vanessa, popped up on the video scene and Kobe slid off with his one, true, and only wife.

Anyhow, I recall around the same time Kobe Bryant came into the league as a rookie I had been taken to a Lakers game against the Warriors held at the Great Western Forum in Inglewood, California where the Lakers had once played. That night I'd seen Kobe without actually seeing Kobe. Again, I wasn't as sports educated as I am today, to have understood back then, now as an early teenager, the hype around Kobe. For one, a skilled enough player to bypass college and go straight into the pros out of high school, drafted at the age of seventeen. Analyzing it now but seeing it from the perspective of the gang culture I was more adapted to at the time in '96, the draft of Kobe would have been like getting put on the set and advancing straight to balling with the sack or off a hundred thousand dollars or better liqk, and immediately having status while only sixteen to eighteen years of age. Skip past all the other new-booties that just got put on, and some of those already on the set but still curb serving or hitting bullshit liqks and splitting crumbs to bubble; then all the hood rats joking and the good girls going against their morals and principles taught about dating or falling in love with a lok; everything I slide through in is clean, on gold or shiny chrome, and I'm g'd up fresh all the time. Plus the OGs in the game before me all give me props. You either have to be from, or understand, the street/gang culture of LA to follow along here. I'm not breaking it down any further. But I hope that you don't miss a great story. Feel me?

But anyway, there he was, Kobe, sitting courtside rows down below me, on the bench but looking eager to get on the court and showcase his talent. And still, I was more focused on Nick Van Exel and Eddie Jones. Two of the proven stars of the Lakers at the time. Now, twenty-three years later, that day serves me as one of those times in your life where you later want to, or do, kick yourself in the ass for. Because after the game that night Kobe was readily hand signing his autograph to whatever. And I literally walked eight feet past the man with a basketball in my hand to chase an autograph from Nick Van Exel, which I never received.

Although, let's keep it real. Who would have honestly known for certain, but for Kobe himself, that I'd passed up on the autograph of a future Hall of Famer? But even more so a four-time NBA All-Star MVP, Sports and World icon, NBA five-times champion, two-times finals MVP, who played twenty seasons and made NBA All-Star eighteen times; was a superstar athlete, two-time Olympic Gold medalist, beloved husband and father, brother and son, author and entrepreneur? Obviously not me. But I'm willing to bet that I'm not alone here. You probably kicked yourself in the ass, too. This Shit Crazy!

One day I pull up to my homeboys Big Snoop and Lil Snoop's spot in my 1986 Oldsmobile Cutlass on stock rims, chipped paint, straight bucket; it's what I drove at the time. Even the driver door was jammed permanently shut. And I had the two door model. So there was only the passenger door to enter and exit from; a very dangerous hazard. Still, I was back and forth from San Bernardino, my mom's house, to LA in this hooptie of mine I'd paid six hundred dollars for. My homeboy Baby Rico used to joke and say, "You made it to the set from San Bernardino in that ugly bitch?" Then point at my car as though it couldn't drive around the block eight times without falling apart. I would just smile or laugh along but defend my wheels like, "Watch out, crim! My hoop run." Shy I was, but not embarrassed. As a point proven, I would pick up girls I dated in this car. And every girl would have to wait her turn to climb in after me before we went somewhere. And I'd have to wait my turn to climb out. Yeah, those were the days of THA L'OK.

Inside the spot, game two of the first round of the playoffs was on TV and setting up to start. Lil Snoop, and the big homies Butchman and Queek, along with a few other heads, were all present to watch the game. There were even a couple bucket heads (ugly or average females) in attendance, hanging out. Which wasn't a surprise to see at the spot. Lil Snoop kept a bucket head around. Though these types of bucket heads did have a car, or job, or their own place—you know, the hood baby momma types. But now he's married to our homegirl Rosy a.k.a. ugly-ass Sharelle (no coincidence there). But only I can call her that and not get T'd off on. I love you Sharelle.

Anyway, when I first arrived I could hear Butchman say, "Hey loved one, let me hit that bud," as I stood outside the steel screen door and knocked for entry. I could also hear the crowd inside. Quickly I tucked away a small dime bag of chronic I had palmed in my hand and planned on smoking with Lil Snoop or Big Snoop, on some kick it with the older homies vibe! Me being the little homey I would often make it a point to show my appreciation to those that helped lace my chucks (raise me) along the way. But right then was bad timing with there being so many heads present. Butchman and Queek would have been straight if it was just them two extra; plus they were G homies. But the other four or five heads I could hear inside as well; naw'h.

There was no point in having my small bag sucked up and gone before it got back around to me to hit a second time. I'd be trying to hit less than a roach you can pinch with two fingers with all them lungs present. "I'll catch back up with Lil Snoop another time," I thought then. Besides, they were all smoking already anyhow. The smoke session had begun. All I needed to do was fall in and play smooth; smoke for free. Not that it was my intention because truly I didn't smoke weed except occasionally—the same as today. However, prior to then I had learned to fall in and hold tight till the blunt or joint came my way. I picked it up from my homeboy Tiny Spoon and my homegirl Orange Flag big ass. The two were pros at it way super back in the day when you had to have five on it, or at least something, to hit the weed. But you didn't have a brown penny to spend at the time. They each finessed the technique of how to still end up hitting the weed for free. You know how it goes; either remain silent and casual until the blunt just so happens to slip your way. Or talk and laugh your way into it. Almost always a laughing smile works. I have a cousin named Dragon or Ogee that ha ha's into hitting the weed for free so swell, that even if you called him on it he'll still somehow laugh, joke, and talk his way into hitting the weed with nothing but a smile or laugh put on it. Facts. It works. Even his brother Cartoon has it down pat. And they both get it from Debra, their mother. Shit runs in the family.

As the game gets underway, to finally tip off, but a time out commercial break comes before, a sudden and loud debate erupts. By now I've hit the weed and I am high at a mellow altitude. But the loudness and aggression in the tone of the voices arguing puts me on alert; or starts the paranoia. Whatever the case, I'm tuned in now. Or maybe I was dozing off because then I yawn and stretch, and I'm half laid back with my eyes closed on the single bed of this small single room house. Weed does me like that sometimes. That's why I'm not a fan of smoking unless I am indoors and completely relaxed beforehand.

Anyhow, as I am listening I pick up that the conversation is about which team is going to win and which isn't. I quickly note that there's a Laker hater present, and who has a loud bark. Each debater starts pointing out individual player skill sets, personal stats, and then the match-ups; onto each team's stats in prior wins or losses during the regular season, to who's trash, or who won by luck. I must say, sport trash talk is entertaining. It is part of the reason I am a fan of sports. Sport trash talk is the humor side of sports. Especially when there are animated characters doing the trash talking. Like these two.

"Cuz, bet! Fuck all this talking. My money on Shaq down in the paint."
Then: "On Hoova, what 'chu try'nuh bet?"
"Bet whatever."
"Bet!"

I finally look around to see who these two are. I had to. It had got exciting. But I wasn't familiar with either.

The two begin reaching into their pants pockets, and one even down into his sock. I was really keen into it now. Then the game came back on and the starting five from each team were standing at center court.

"Stop slow dragging, groove. You see the game coming on."
"Shit you ain't pulled nothing out neither."

They put one another on blast—on the spot. I can tell the bluff went too far. But then…

"Here! Bet two hooves."

"Bet! I think I have two dollars."

"Wow," I say to myself. Now I don't have a wooden nickel in the bet, being that sports isn't all the way my thing just yet. So I'm chilling and being a spectator actually. However, the way these two just carried on I expected they would at least bet a hundred dollars; if not a million or a trillion. But hey, that's sports for you. And I was slowly being drawn closer and closer back into its culture. This Shit Crazy!

After leaving Lil Snoop's spot, I bent a couple corners to check a few traps. I spot and pull on one of my functional custos named Kirk. He owes me a few dollars but pays good and so I'm not sweating it. I wouldn't have stopped but for him flagging me down.

I park, get out, and meet Kirk standing beside his own car.

"Boy, Youngsta, where've you been?" asks Kirk with mild excitement.

Kirk addresses me by the name I use with the fiends on the block I sell to. But I can see that Kirk is feeling himself about something.

"What's up?" I reply while keeping an eye on the street and all the traffic as a precaution.

Kirk grins. "I wasn't trying to spend with no one else; plus I owe you something. You always take care of me."

Kirk then digs into his pockets and pulls out a small knot. I can only imagine how much of it has shrunk in the time span of him looking for me to now him finally catching up with me.

"I have the twenty I owe you; and I'm looking to spend twenty-five with you."

"Damn," I say to myself and take a closer look at Kirk while simultaneously tonguing the inside of my mouth. Kirk, dressed in a pair of gym shorts, a T-shirt, and a hat that all have Lakers emblems depicted on them, looks so fresh and so clean; minus the big beads of sweat glazing his brow. "Yeah, he been smoking good," I conclude. But then I look and peep the fanny pack around his waist with Lakers on it too. And freshly new. The only items on him that don't have Lakers logos somewhere on them are his socks and shoes.

Kirk peels me off a fifty and tells me to keep the change. I spit three plastic wrapped crack rocks into my empty palm like I'm coughing and pass them through a dap.

"O'l school, check you out. You then hit a liqk huh? I see you champ; Lakers out the game too," I say with a chuckle.

"Every day I'm hustling; some days better than others. I'm trying to put some extra money in your pocket too. And not from this shit neither." Kirk says, referring to the drugs I just sold him.

"How so?" I reply while stuffing the fifty in my pocket. But now my interest is piqued.

"Investing. Take some of the money you're making and go into business with me. See, check it out!"

Kirk pops the three rocks I just gave him into his mouth then turns and opens the back passenger door of his car. Inside on the seat there are about thirty new T-shirts laid out all with Lakers emblems on them. But still, I don't get it.

"Alright, so what's up?" I respond.

Kirk points. "I sell these T-shirts twenty dollars profit, each. I buy them wholesale at seven dollars each. Do the math. That's thirteen dollars profit, each."

"I feel you." My brow shrinks with expression.

"Yeah? Well come with me tomorrow and I'll take you downtown. You can buy you some shirts to sell for the next game. We'll go down to the Staples Center, set up, and sell out stock. Easy money. I just did it today," revealed Kirk.

The wheels in my head began turning. Though not how they should have. I should have been all over this like a sweet liqk. But I wasn't.

Naturally I'm a hustler at heart. Since eight years of age I have touched money or merchandise some way somehow. At twelve I made and counted my first five hundred dollars. By seventeen I bought my first car. And on and on. Still, this felt different; almost awkward. This hustle Kirk presented me with required me to stand out in a parking lot or at a corner light holding T-shirts out to motorists and spectators heading to watch the game, or simply a fan of the Lakers passing in traffic but willing to support the hustle. I don't know why, but I felt skeptical about the matter. I mean, I was pretty much already doing this same routine selling drugs. But now home court would be different, on top of the hustle being different. I wasn't feeling sure. And it showed.

Kirk exhaled with patience. "Listen. Just buy some shirts, invest your money. Then come with me to the Staples Center and I'll sell the shirts for you, Youngsta. Just so you can see that there's a way to hustle in these streets but be legit. The police won't mess with you, and you don't have to be on constant alert like how on the block with all this gangbanging going on around here. Also, you can experience the Lakers Nation. It'll have you bleeding purple and gold."

Then Kirk paused and peered at me, how a father looks his son over, an uncle his nephew, or grandfather his grandson.

He said. "Well look, if I'm registering to you; meet me here in the morning no later than eight. I'm not going to hold you up tonight, or myself. I'm about to finish enjoying the night off.

"But listen now, the opportunity will drive off at eight-o-one. No later. Be safe tonight." Then Kirk climbed into his car and left.

And I was left with a choice to make.

Chapter 2

Every Day I'm Hustling

The next day I met up with Kirk and invested seven hundred dollars of the thousand I had to my name, for one hundred T-shirts. Fuck it; why not? A hustle is a hustle. A liqk is a liqk. And this one made sense after thinking it over. At the end of the day I'd profit thirteen hundred dollars and, as Kirk said, not have to look over my shoulder.

I recall around this same time, a different O'l head who worked at a school I attended (YOU) as the janitor, twice pulled me up about investing. I had stood out to him amongst the majority of the other students because of my dress and shoe game. My homeboy Baby H-Crazy (Raymond Coon Jr.) had put me onto a clothing store on the eastside, and another one in Downtown LA, that both sold popular brand urban wear at the time and at a discount, though some of the clothes were knock offs. Still, and for almost a month straight I wore a fresh fit with a nice pair of shoes each time I stepped on the school campus.

I remember the janitor pulling me to the side and saying, "Say, not to be in your business but I see you, young man. You dress nice. And I doubt that it's your parents that are keeping you fresh." He would pause to see whether or not I'd interject. I didn't. He continued.

"Do you know about stocks and investing? You can take some of the money you're making—obviously, however you're making it, I'm not in your business, but invest the money rather than buying clothes and shoes. Meet me after school and we can go somewhere so I can teach you how."

I had heard a little about what stocks and bonds were and could find the section of the newspaper that read about it, but I knew nothing about how any of it worked. And here I was, nineteen years of age. Still, I'd respond that I knew a little about stocks, and I'd give the impression that I would fall behind after school to meet up with him. However, once school ended for the day, all studying and learning ended for the day as well. I went straight to the block and to do what I knew best at the time. Ignorantly so. Now sometimes when I think back on it, like right now, I kick myself in the ass. But at the same time, back then, people I had met in my life like the janitor are why I took Kirk up on his offer later.

I go with Kirk to the Staples Center. I decide not to let him do all the hustling himself. But instead I join in for the experience and activity. So there I was alongside Kirk, dressed in Lakers paraphernalia: shirt and wrist band for me. Kirk had a similar getup, from a couple days before: shirt, hat, shorts, and fanny pack. Just the addition of a wrist band like mine, and a pair of socks with the Lakers logo on them he'd found and had to have when we were downtown for the shirts and merchandise. Anyhow, we take post at a few entries of the Staples Center parking lot gates, and a light corner or two. However, on two separate instances we had to beat out competition (a different vendor hand-hustling too) for vacant posts. And of one of these two times led to Kirk having a verbal fight over what was considered a prime location. Kirk hadn't mentioned beforehand how things could get territorial. He was out there beefing for sales like how some hustlers do on the block. I didn't know whether to get cracc'n or stay cool. It was funny out there.

At the end of the day, though, I had only but nineteen shirts left. Not bad. But I would never go again after that day to hustle that way; out in the open, under the sun and sweating, plus competing and beefing with civilians for posts and sales. The experience overall was cool, but just not for me. Although, and still, I later thanked Kirk for the game and opportunity he afforded me. He appreciated that and took the remaining nineteen shirts off of me at ten dollars each. I was cool with that; even slid three dime rocks on the strength of him exposing me to his hustle and the outing we'd shared. That memory is now priceless. Because I had not only been initiated further into the Lakers culture, but back into the culture of sports overall. As a kid I was a pre-fan of sports, but then somewhere as a teen I lost interest, until later in my early twenties I renewed and sealed my interest for life. I'll elaborate more on that point later.

Prior to my experience with Kirk, but which also somewhat factored into my decision to hustle the T-shirts with him, I recall a time my Uncle Fred took me and my cousin Casey Jr. to an LA Clippers home game. This was back when the Clipps played at the LA Sports Arena and Danny Manning, before he turned out a bust after starring big in college, played for the city's underdog. But for argument's sake, Danny suffered a career ending injury.

Anyhow, during that evening and after eating at a diner called Bill's Tacos before going to the game, while inside the parking lot of the LA Sports Arena, I witnessed LA Clippers wear being sold. Now fast forward to the experience with Kirk; I figured if a LA Clippers T-shirt, and other things like that, could sell in the early 1990s and the Clipps hadn't won anything but a winning regular season and a playoff game at best, then certainly the logo of the Lakers on anything in 2002, when they were coming off two consecutive championship seasons and were now in the first round of the playoffs, would definitely sell. That much I did understand about sports and a winning home team.

Or later seeing a profit where a liqk laid. And not to mention a home team with the duo of Shaquille O'Neal and Kobe Bryant on the roster to inspire the grind in me.

That night at the LA Sports Arena I recall my uncle having us seats right alongside Danny Manny's father and grandfather, or some significant elders of his. Though I personally had not initially known who it was we were sitting next to high up in the stands. And who I'd borrowed a set of binoculars from to see closer to the court. Not until I called Danny Manny trash for missing a few buckets did the news become known to me. My uncle, who had been carrying on a conversation with the two gentlemen, had already learned who they were. And so when I blurted out my blasphemy he popped me something swift to the back of my head, then informed me of the news. I was around ten years of age, but no older than eleven then.

I apologized afterwards. But after that night, strangely enough, the LA Clippers became my home team underdog to root for a win. Even over the purple and gold. Yeah, that's right. Read back a few pages, I never said, *I* was a Lakers fan. Though I wouldn't dare pick the LA Clippers, of any era, over the Shaq and Kobe era with the Lakers. Maybe not even the Kobe, Casol, Meta World Peace, Lamar Odom era either.

But now this is the 2019–2020 season. I love Kawhi Lenard, Paul George (not so much), Lou Williams and the LA Clippers over LeBron James, Anthony Davis, Raja Ronda (a dog at the point guard position), and the LA Lakers. COVID-19 fucked up some good match-ups, and competition overall, this year, in the world of sports. Especially for Olympians, being that the Olympics is held only every four years. And 2020 was the scheduled year to compete. That's a lot of training, work ethic, and build-up in anticipation to then not be able to compete. Trust me, I get it. However, the world is suffering under a health crisis. And safety is a priority, right? Though the NBA might resume later. Most sports leagues and pretty much anything going on, at least in the U.S., is discontinued for now.

Anyway, and truthfully, I don't have any particular favorite team over all else in sports. I more or less have good-to-great players and team rosters I favor. Like the Kobe, Shaq, and Lakers three rings roster; CP3, De'Andre Jordan, Blake Griffin's run with the Clipps or Barron Davis, Eldan Brand, and Sam Cecil's run before that group; Steve Nash, Shawn Marion, Amari Staudimier and the Phoenix Suns' 2007 roster; oh, and I loved the Golden State Warriors' entire roster. The one before KD arrived, when the bench was deep; the 2014–2015 and 2015–2016 rosters.

It is not even arguable that that roster is the truest built-from-the-ground-up championship team; that Coach Mark Jackson initially helped put together, of all the teams that won a chip in the new millennium; aside from a San Antonio Spurs team the great Popovich put together. For the Golden State, no player on its roster was a superstar or All-Star before arriving in Oakland and going on to win a ring against Bron-Bron and the Cavs. Then repeating the next year before losing in game 7 by a bucket to Kyrie Erving and the Cavs. I purposely distinguished the leading name on the loss or victory for the Cavs because Kyrie gained the victory and LeBron never beat Golden State without Kyrie. Facts.

Players such as the following are my favorites! Dirk Nowitzki, Spud Webb, Chris Paul, Larry Bird, Charles Barkley, Shaquille O'Neal, Dennis Rodman, Allen Iverson, Steven Nash, Kobe Bryant, Shawn Marion, Kevin Durant. And last but not least, 'that dude' Barron Davis. Although I didn't know Barron Davis personally, I nevertheless attended the same elementary school as him, South Park Elementary, on the eastside of South LA at the same time he did.

Many years after, and once it became known to me through watching a documentary that this star athlete was a South Central LA native, and he'd attended the same school as I did, I questioned myself whether or not I too could have made it playing sports. I was good at playing football; my number one go-to and favorite sport as a kid. I could accurately throw a football and catch one too. But I swear that now, it's like I never had any talent in football whatsoever. I can't throw a football and can hardly catch one; I'm straight garbage. Though I'm sure that it's a mind thing, from a lack of practice and activity in the sport.

Back when I took to the streets as an adolescent teen, gangbanging and hustling became my mental and actively physical sport. It was either you're in the streets, or you're staying behind after school or somewhere else to play sports and hopefully someday make it big from doing so. And I wasn't reared enough to stay after school. Or influenced by the peers I ran with to do so.

For most back then, if you were repping a set, then you were in the set hanging and banging all day. There wasn't a big promotion or expectation in the hood for you to excel in sports or academics coming from your peers, or even family, the way it is today. Not in my hood at least. Sports or academics were considered for squares. But today, the choice of either-or is obsolete to a great degree. You can rep your set and go ball in sports as a professional and be promoted, reared, and expected to do so from your family and peers back in the hood. It's not an "Oh, you a square," thing anymore. The hood mentality or gang culture is more receptive and embracing of a homeboy or homegirl making it out of the hood and excelling at whatever, while still be appreciated and respected in the hood. As are national sports leagues or corporate America on the flip side, better receptive or embracing of a talented prospect coming out from the hood and showcasing his or her talent, making corporate dollars, but still associated intimately with the hood. Had this been the all-around culture, from the hood to Wall Street, twenty or thirty years ago there would have been a lot more athletes in the league, or successful life stories period, from the hoods all throughout the nation. But thankfully that has evolved.

A look now around every national pro league in sports reveals a kid from the hood repping it proudly. And if you've spent time in prison before or just know someone who has, or who is doing time now, then you know that there are pro-type athletes all over the prison yards, where the culture of sports is essential to an inmate's level of sanity. Without being able to watch, read, listen to, or play sports some people incarcerated would lose their minds to boredom. Which brings me back to how I later became fully invested in sports and grew to have a genuine love for the Black Mamba.

Chapter 3

Sports & Culture

Once I took to the streets, at the early age of twelve, sports were no longer an activity I was intimately involved with. I even stopped collecting pro sports trading cards, something I once loved doing. It would keep me busy for hours at a time. I had a good two three-ring binder books filled with plastic sleeves of basketball, baseball, and football cards; though I recall having three or four hockey cards in the mix too. This was in the early 1990s and when I lived with my grandmother Alice Williams for a short period. It was me and five other of her grandkids plus her nephew, my cousin Mark, living in the house. He was the oldest at about fourteen. We would all get a weekly or bi-weekly allowance, and with the five dollars she gave me I would at least spend two of it buying a pack of Tops or Upper Deck trade/collection cards.

For two years I collected hundreds of cards. I kept my book arranged in sections by each sport and kept the rookie players cards of each sport classified separately. I recall having rookie cards of: QB-Bret Farve, QB-Troy Aikman, WR-Jerry Rice, RB-Emmit Smith or maybe it was RB-Barry Sanders. It was one of the two. I also had a rookie card for Spud Webb, and Larry Johnson a.k.a. Grandmama for the Charlotte Hornets then. I also had cards, but not rookie season, of the Houston Astro's pitcher Nolan Ryan, the LA Dodgers' Darryl Strawberry, the Seattle Mariners' Kenneth Griffin Jr. and other big names or baseball Hall of Famers. I also collected a separate binder book of Marvel Comic cards.

Thinking back on all that now, I miss those days. I had even learned the business profit side of collecting cards and kept me a Becketts book to follow the stock of each card collected that held value. I guess you can say that was my first initiation into stock and trade investing. And I used to do a lot of it. But then one day I left all my card binder books by accident inside a friend of a family member's car, never to see them again. I was around the age ten or eleven now and had been staying back with my mom. Ooh, was I mad, and for months afterwards.

First I was mad at myself; how could I be so absent minded to leave my card books in the back seat of some guys car? How stupid of me. I had carried those card books around with me that entire day, I remember. Then my mom and I got a ride somewhere, or no, we had spent some days over at a family member's house and later were getting a ride home or something. The point is all of a sudden I forgot my cards and didn't think of them until the old man whose car we were in went driving off and had turned the corner. Damn. Second I was later mad that my mom didn't do more to get my cards back. I had grown attached to the whole activity of collecting, buying, and trading. I can honestly say that the loss of those cards played a pivotal role in my later statement of *forget sports*. Then afterwards being drawn more to the streets as an alternate activity.

Looking back at that moment in my life, I would advise today that anyone who is raising a child, or just knows one whose mind is fully invested in a task that is productive or that can possibly later lead to something great—invest in that kid's thoughts. Help keep his or her mind occupied with that specific goal, hobby, or activity. Because if that child loses interest, like an undisciplined adult, there is no telling what their mind might become attracted to next. In my case, it went all bad. But first, I begged the ear off of my mom about those cards. I can still hear her get agitated and say, "Boy leave me alone about them damn cards. Go find something else to do!" And eventually I did. The streets.

Not until I started getting arrested and doing time did I grow an interest in sports again. My first arrest was at the age of twelve, and again when I was thirteen. Which is when I was sent to a prison camp for juveniles. And no, not a camp out in the woods where you tell ghost stories at night around a campfire. This was a jail facility. The movie *Grid Iron* starring Dwayne 'The Rock' Johnson and rapper Xzibit depicts the prison camp quite precisely. And it is a true story that I closely relate to. So closely that when I recently watched it in 2018 for the first time I nearly cried a tear. And that's a lot for me. But the storyline hit close to home.

Anyhow, the juvenile delinquent system reignited my active interest in playing sports. Though not until my adulthood did I actually start watching and studying to learn sports; growing an emotional feel for the culture. But still, I credit that to being incarcerated. Can the incarcerated get a shout out one time every now and then from the networks ESPN, NFL Network, NBA TV, TNT, MLB Live, NHL Network, and so on? The convicted support the hell out of sports. You hear me Stephen A. Smith, Max Kellerman, and First Takes, the Jump, Highly Questionable? And all the rest. I mean damn, can us brothas get some love. This Shit Crazy!

A week after I went and sold those Lakers T-shirts with Kirk, I caught a gun possession charge. So I missed the rest of the Playoffs, the Western and Eastern conference finals, and later the NBA Finals: the Los Angeles Lakers versus the New Jersey Nets. However, I was able to follow the headlines of the games by newspaper, telephone, and word of mouth. And lo and behold, the LA Lakers had won it all again. Funny thing is, as the Lakers kept advancing from series to series, periodically I would think and say to myself, "Boy, I would have come up selling those T-shirts," and "I bet Kirk probably out there blowing like a broke stove with all the money he making if he still hustling."

I did roughly five months in LA Men's Central County Jail, before I was released in late August or early September of 2002. And still the City was celebrating the Lakers' back to back to back championships. And already fans were predicting a four-peat. The Lakers' Nation's ego was huge; it had me scheming to invest in T-shirts again. I even thought about Kirk, who I never ran back into ever again. I don't even know if my o'l school part'na is still living today. If he is, it would be nice to kick back and watch a game with him once I am released. For the culture of the game if nothing more.

The fall out between Shaq and Kobe, and all the press about teammates accusing Kobe of not being a team player, and a hotdog with the ball, made me scrutinize the Black Mamba. Then Coach Phil Jackson publicly stated along the lines that Kobe was uncoachable. That really made me look at the picture there. Upon closer observation during the

Lakers games I'd watch, I too began to form the opinion that Kobe was one arrogant brat and a hot-dogging motha-fuk shut yo' mouth. For real. And so for years after I used to ride his name bad in sports debates. Especially during a game I'm watching, and I see Kobe try to drive to the hole with the opposing team's entire starting five guarding him plus an extra defender off the bench, while three of his teammates are spotted up open and calling for the ball; instead Kobe spins and shoots a fallaway that hits all iron. Then what Kobe do, he looks around but at no one and gets back on defense as though "What? Shit happens." And on the very next possession call for the ball adamantly. Now I know I exaggerated about the six defenders on the court, but I'm not far from telling the truth.

Anyhow, even a little after Kobe performed in winning two titles without Shaq I still sometimes would criticize that it didn't *prove* he could win without Shaq, when the debate would be that he did. Because the mastermind who assembled both prior and present championship rosters on the court was always Coach Phil Jackson to begin with, as well as the triangle offense he ran effectively that other NBA teams and coaches in a game series could not rally or close out a defeat against. A fact, and truly the only fact proven. Before Phil Jackson joined the Lakers as head coach, Kobe and Shaq were already there and hadn't won a title. And without Phil Jackson, neither Kobe nor the Lakers organization in the 2000 millennium had or has won a title thus far. You can have the best player in the league or all the talent you want on a team, but if there isn't a coach involved who can organize it, then what team in all sports has won a title? Enlighten me. That there would be my comeback in every debate, whether right or wrong, when centered around one great talent who was being claimed to have won a title without another great talent that they previously won a title with, and as if the other great talent suddenly now upon victory didn't make a difference before. And so too I would scrutinize Kobe's talent like, "Yeah his game is definitely superb; but he's trash if he can't play team ball or with another great talent in a team sport. Win, lose, or draw." Now I say that about all highly talented players with arrogant selfish-type egos in any team sport: Kyrie Irving at one point in time, Russell Westbrook most certainly, John Wall and a couple others in the NBA. Antonio Brown, Odell Beckham Jr. to name a couple in the NFL. So on and so on throughout team ball in sports; it takes a team to beat a team. That's basic knowledge.

When it was being rumored that Shaq and Kobe's differences had reached a breaking point and the two were no longer able to play another season together, the front office needed to make a decision, or at least that's the expression I recall having; I'm not going to lie, I wanted Shaq to stay, and Kobe to catch a plane or bus elsewhere. But that was purely based on the game the way that I understood it at the time in the leagues. Shaq was the number one big man at the center's position. He almost couldn't be denied a bucket down in the paint unless hacked or held. I don't know what his percentage was in the paint, but I clearly recall the ideal was to just get the ball to him up high or down low and he would do the rest. Don't sweat it. Against whoever. And on the flip side, I felt like Kobe at shooting guard could be replaced with let's say at the time: a healthy Penny Hardaway, a Reggie Miller, or fit AI in at that position since Kobe felt AI was the hardest guard he had to defend, let Phil Jackson teach any of them the triangle offense alongside Shaq, and it was butter for a title. I could be wrong, though. But the point is there was only one Shaquille O'Neal in the league. And he was he: himself.

So when Shaq left I was like the Lakers is through-vo, over with, ka'bishe. And then when he won a title I believe his second year down in South Beach with 'The Man' Dwayne Wade, I felt the fact was well proven: from a win-loss, great talent, team ball perspective, where one great talent teams up with another great talent and gets the job done.

Obviously many, if not all at that point around the NBA culture, also felt that the Lakers had made a bad choice in not getting Shaq to stay. Then too, Phil Jackson had stepped away as coach for the Lakers. It went downhill quick for the purple and gold. So fast that Kobe finally threw a tantrum and demanded to be traded. Especially with all the media rubbing in Shaq's success in winning fourth ring title he gained with the Miami Heat, while questioning Kobe about his own lack of success. Though out of all the drama that escalated in the years after Shaq and Phil Jackson left the Lakers and before Phil Jackson later returned, Kobe gracefully matured. Because so I then began to learn a valuable gem about human character from the Black Mamba. And which I grew to respect him for, and crown him the greatest player of my generation on and off the court.

Envy, jealousy, and hate are all one thing, each their own entity. Competitiveness is entirely different. To envy is to despise another for having something you want but cannot have, or don't know how to achieve, or someone for being who they are or what you are not or do not know how to be or to become. Jealousy is to harbor resentment towards someone enjoying something, especially when you are not. And hate is both envy and jealousy together that forms malice in the heart.

On the other hand, competitiveness, within the act or mindset of competing, can appear as envy, jealously, or hate. However, the difference is there is no malice in the heart in true competitiveness, outside of the competition, in American sports. To want the exact same title or win an opponent is competing for or has won is a part of the game. Competition. To not want to see a rival opponent or nemesis with a title or win you cannot possibly have or have achieved already is also a part of the game, within the grudge of competition—to hate your opponent or competitive rival in competition, and never wish them any success as long as they're your nemesis, is too plain competitiveness in the context of active sports. But that is the world of sports; a part of the game.

Red Sox vs. Yankees, Dodgers vs. Giants; Celtics vs. Knicks, Michael Jordan and the Chicago Bulls vs. Isaiah Thomas and the "Bad Boys" Detroit Pistons, Magic Johnson and the Lakers vs. Larry Bird and the Celtics; Kenny Stabler and the Oakland Raiders vs. Terry Bradshaw and the Pittsburgh Steelers, Francis Tarkington and the Vikings vs. Roger Staubach and the Cowboys. These are all historical teams and players who were rivals in a competitive sport that hated one another on the field or court during competition. And the same can be found on the ice in hockey or on the field in soccer or probably in the pool with water polo for Christ's sake. I'm not that educated yet. But is this attitude of competing right—conscientiously? Maybe not, or absolutely no. Sports can be enjoyed or appreciated without all the contempt, violence, or anger, in my and I'm sure others' opinion. But is it the attitude of the game played and loved by fans and players both? Yes. 1000%.

Kobe Bryant's personality on the court within the game of basketball had the attributes of envy, jealousy, and hate. Or from a different angle, it was more like selfishness, being inconsiderate, plus stubborn pride. Either way, it still is in the context of competition and competitiveness. He was one competitive individual. Just take a critical look at who he openly idolized in the game of basketball: Michael Jordan—competitive, arrogant, zealous, who played to dethrone his opponent, and who hated to lose big games. Especially to the "Bad Boys" Detroit Pistons, his arch nemeses.

When it was said that Kobe envied Shaq's leadership on the team, or his charisma with their teammates in and out of the locker room, or was jealous of Shaq winning a championship before he himself again won a title, it turned out to be pure competitiveness. But when I didn't see it from the proper perspective, that it was aggressive competitiveness, I admittedly formed a bad opinion of Kobe. Not until afterwards did I truly accept the nature of sports played, its aggressive-competitiveness side, and the primary objective to always win, did my perspective on Kobe's attitude and personality change.

Initially I grew up playing sports to naturally have competitive fun. Not for wins or losses. I then later learned to be aggressively competitive. There is a huge difference there. One is pure (competitive fun). The other is or can be toxic (aggressive competitiveness). It is why I state that, not until after I "accepted" the aggressive nature of sports did my perspective of Kobe change. Once I started being aggressively-competitive in life I too began to hate to lose or see my opponent or nemesis win without feeling envy or jealousy. I don't say this today to say that it is a good thing, now that I bought into the concept, because truthfully it is not.

Having competitive fun is one thing, and pure. But being aggressively-competitive can be toxic, and has a downside which ultimately is an emotional roller coaster that I'm sure can be traced to instances where it has mentally and physically ruined or badly affected plenty of people; their lives, relationships, and opportunities. The entire concept that only one can win, be the best, and so forth, in an aggressive competition is a malicious one. Because technically, our social ideology doesn't have to be to compete against one another. But hey, we live in a society that is all about competition. That's capitalism for you. So get aggressive if you plan to win.

Anyhow, after I adopted and grew into this vying and predatory behavior, I became aggressively competitive at everything I played or did that required me to win: sports, playing video games, table top games, board games, to hustling and making money or even learning something and teaching myself new things that the next person might not know or that I wasn't expected by others to learn or accomplish. I was even competitive about making a woman have an orgasm before I did during sex. Like for a spell that became a sport.

However, when I didn't win at any of these things I have mentioned, or whatever else I set my mind to aggressively compete at, and I'd lose, then it became the only time where all the thoughts and emotions of hate, envy, or jealousy and so on would stir up in me as though a sudden curse had befallen me. And now most times I wish I hadn't ever adopted that aggressively-competitive mentality. Like, it serves me greatly at times because of the society today. But again, the downside to it is a volcano mud slide or avalanche snowing down on you. It will bury you alive. I caution teaching a child or any adult this mentality. It takes a lot to handle it properly.

I recall when I used to play basketball, long before I stopped engaging in the activity here in prison, I would play with intense emotions. And if I lost a game sometimes, my hang-up would show in the heated fits I would catch. But then one day in the year 2006 while incarcerated at MDC-LA and after a game of basketball I'd lost, an associate at the time, Trevonne 'Trey' Mitchell, who claimed to be a close friend of NFL pro wide receiver Keyshawn Johnson, said to me before leaving the small half court: "On Avalon! Cuz you always talking about Kobe being a sore sport-loser, or hot-dogging, or a hater; you need to take a look in the mirror. Stop hating because you lost a game. Now you don't want to talk to nobody."

But that wasn't the case. And I would definitely dispute the accusation that I was a hater because I lost a game, and now I didn't want to be friends or talk to anybody. However, I eventually had to stop, think, and evaluate the entire situation, and similar scenarios. My famous response to being called a hater or accused of envying was, "I'm not in competition with anyone to then hate or envy!" Although I couldn't articulate how so, especially when my actions of anger or shutting a person out and so on contradicted me. Even still, I knew in my heart that outside of the game of aggressive competition I personally didn't have an issue with anyone I competed against. But if so, it derived from the game.

After considering all the above: the aggressive-competitiveness of sports, emotions, wins or losses, and so on, but including how I initially and naturally played sports for competitive fun, I reasoned that if I can honestly say that I am not a hater, or envious of anything or anyone, and that I'm not in competition with anyone outside of a competitive game, then—that's when it dawned on me that neither was Kobe. He was only in competition within the game for the goal and objective to win a title and also to be great at it. He was not in competition with any particular individual per se, including Shaq. It was merely the fact that an individual might stand in the way of his goal or objective to obtain a win or achieve greatness in an aggressively-competitive sport. From this new perspective, I began to keenly watch, learn from, and respect the Black Mamba: his intuitive thinking, his overall personality, his drive and objective on and off the court.

I watched an interview Kobe did post career, the one I believe where he's walking through his personal gallery? He spoke about his career, achievements, and his present and future plans moving forward. That's when I later learned the man had genius DNA in him. I really then truly became his biggest supporter and fan.

When people speak or debate the meaning of killer instinct, I like to agree that it is having a natural or easily activated aggressive-competitiveness, to be good at what you do and win without showing any compassion for your opponent(s) during the moment of competition. Athletes such as Michael Jordan, Kobe Bryant, Serena Williams, Mike Tyson, Floyd Mayweather Jr., Russell Westbrook, LeBron James, Tony Hawk, or Coach Bill Belichick; artists such as Dr. Dre, Ice Cube, Jay-Z, Nipsy Hussle, 50 Cent, 2Pac, Master P. Miller; and business moguls Donald J. Trump, Oprah, and Martha Stewart to randomly name a few, all have that aggressive-competitiveness that serves as killer instinct. Whether natural or easily activated, when it's show time they each, within their respective professions, undeniably dominate or have dominated opponents and or objectives on the court or field, in the ring, in the boardroom, in media or the music industry, or on Wall Street. I humbly idolize the upside to aggressive-competitiveness in each of these individuals plus their remarkable success in history.

When it comes to the killer instinct trait, I don't believe everyone is born with it, or surely it's not activated. But I do believe that many who are gifted with a natural aggressive-competitiveness to serve for a great cause in life, unfortunately pass on before ever identifying with or activating this killer instinct within them to serve humanity. And sadly so.

Kobe Bryant was not only an athlete but also a philanthropist and mentor. His killer instinct or aggressively-competitive upside to attack, dominate, and overwhelm an opposition didn't just serve to dethrone or deprive opponents of their chance to win or retain titles, but off the court his intelligence and inquisitiveness was helping to make the world a better place.

Following Kobe's life and career after his retirement from playing ball helped me to further identify with the killer instinct gifted within my own self. I had known it was there but not for the proper reason. Mine didn't or doesn't serve for the cause of playing sports, tabletop games, video games, gangbanging, corner-block-street hustling, or making a woman orgasm before I do. Instead, I discovered I have a killer instinct to lead and organize, protect and serve a body of people. My natural aggressive-competitiveness is for creating solutions that bring forth wealth, order, balance and peace. I now like to think of myself as a king, general, enforcer, and creator. I recall as an adolescent having all these traits but not knowing how to identify with them or bring them out of me. The Black Mamba in part has helped change that.

Chapter 4

I Felt it for Real

When news first broke of Kobe Bryant's death I was here in the cell lying back on the bed doing some constructive thinking and writing. My train of thought was then broken by some dude yelling through his door out and over the tier. But first, he makes the ESPN instrumental intro: *Dunna-na, dunna-na.*

"Kobe Bryant has died this morning in a car crash. *Dunna-na, dunna-na.*"

'Kobe died? Ain't no way!' I thought to myself immediately afterwards. It didn't ring true to me, on top of me knowing how most of these catz around me are so bored and miserable that they'll say something outlandish just for attention. Usually I will dismiss such foolishness before it gets to the point of me having to ignore it. But for some reason hearing that Kobe'd died made me want to get up and yell out the door in response, "Go sit you dumb ass down off the door whoever you are." But again, I was occupied with doing something constructive with my time. Plus I didn't want to start, then indulge in, a bar fight: talking shit from behind the lock-secured door. An act I prohibit myself from doing.

Anyhow, I took the announcement as an obnoxious outburst of nonsense. I'd just not too long before listened to the radio briefly before whoever it was had screamed on the door, and I didn't hear such a thing. I figured too that if something of that magnitude was true then it would be breaking news.

But then thirty minutes later, after the first report, someone else screamed from the door that Kobe was in a crash in LA. Seconds later a chorus of different voices began chiming in to report the same or question the veracity of the tale. Still, I pondered whether it was a joke being hatched for miserable entertainment. It's called inmate-dot-com, where one inmate will intentionally start a rumor just to see how far it spreads and what type of physical reaction it creates.

For instance, an inmate will whisper in the ear of another, "It's about to go on lock-down. A dude over in the other building (way on the other side of the yard) was found nonresponsive in the cell." Then the receiver will take it and pass it to the next and so on until now catz are in a panic scrambling and scurrying about spreading gossip. While grabbing ice, water, food, drugs, and whatever else in preparation for the believed lock-down that is coming. Then you at the same time have those competing to get to the phone or email first to call or email an urgent message to family or friends that the prison is going on lock-down. All this just to see the chain effect of catz running around like chickens with their heads cut off, as entertainment. This is the type of environment I'm in. This Shit Crazy!

Once the chiming began, after I identified who some of the voices belonged to and who wouldn't be playing ignorant games, I said to myself, 'Damn, I gotta tune in to the radio and catch the next half hour report on the local stations.' Being that here at Thomson-ASUP in Illinois, ESPN has been channeled out of sequence now for six months or longer.

But anyhow. 'Was Kobe speeding in one of his Lambos? I always heard of him having and riding around parts of LA in them'

'Is he now on life support, to where it's being speculated that his fate is death rather than survival?'

'They are saying that it was a car crash. People survive that all the time.' All these questions or thoughts, and more, were bouncing around in my head now. This shit really was crazy. Because if true, that Kobe was deceased, then life could be a cold twist.

Welp, life certainly can be a cold twist. I caught the report at the next half hour. But a helicopter crash! That part I wouldn't even have imagined. Nor would I have thought for a second that his daughter Gianna or seven others would perish alongside Kobe. The impact overwhelmed me with hurt, frustration, anger, anxiety, fear, and confusion all at once. Confusion because for a second I questioned whether or not I should be feeling hurt, anger, fear, or anxiety at the intensity I was. From one to ten it was at an eight. Not failing to mention that a case of depression came over me for a spell also. I mean, like, why?

I didn't personally know Kobe, neither did I know Gigi or the others; John, Keri, and their daughter Alyssa Altobelli; Christina Mauser; Sarah and daughter Payton Chester; or the pilot Ara Zobayan. However, it was the compassion for lives ended too soon or so suddenly that touched me. Plus the frightening tragedy, and then my personal respect to a brotha who had made a positive impact in my life while not even knowing me. I idolize that now about Kobe.

Anger is a strong emotion that can serve for both smiles and frowns. There is good anger, and then there is bad anger. But on that afternoon of the crash I was all frowns. Who was the pilot? What was he thinking? Then as the report developed; what was Kobe thinking? All it takes is one bad or miscalculated decision and it can be your last. Later knowledge that the pilot was Kobe's personal pilot gave me the impression that they were deep in discussion when it came to making flight decisions. Therefore on this day, Kobe was well aware and informed about the risk of flying in bad weather conditions, or the attempt to fly at low altitude prior to it being done, but still he trusted his pilot and aircraft. And if this was the case, then it's possible that this wasn't the only time risk had been taken. However, I am only speculating. When frustrated with anger these are the thoughts and questions that weigh heavy on the mind.

As these thoughts and questions burdened me with curiosity, reports or discussions airing on the radio became more frequent. Or better, I couldn't turn the radio off until after hours and so I caught nearly every half hour report. Plus I listened to the Dan Patrick Show. But then what pissed me off is that I didn't hear a deeper hurt in the broadcasters' or commentators' voices, when reporting or commenting on the tragic death of a legend, that I felt I should have heard. Or else it was just me, and I was hurt deeper than I truly realized I was. And so I felt everyone in the world of sports should have been as hurt as Vanessa Bryant.

Later I saw photos published of Vanessa clearly depicting a torn woman, wife, and mother. A statement I read quoted her: "…Life truly isn't fair. This is just senseless," confirming a person that is torn. But even deeper for me it confirms how everyone in life is equal under the surface when it comes to hurt, pain, and grief. No matter how poor or rich, famous or unheard of, the heart is an organ that feels. Even in those that appear cold.

Greatness, relentlessness, and humility solidify the closing chapter of Kobe's honorable legacy as a man, husband, and father; an athlete, champion, and inspiration; a teacher, student, legend, and icon. On the one hand he left us too soon, because of all he had planned and still expected to give his family and the rest of the world through his life that appeared to have ended in tragedy. But not so. On the other hand, clear and divine, the Black Mamba graced us all with God's plan through him and the impact of his legacy and death is a teaching and blessing decreed by the Creator who is in us all. Therefore Kobe's spiritual life and experience in the physical flesh (mundane world) was in fact fulfilled as were all the others that transitioned alongside him from this realm of existence to the next.

Several months after Kobe's passing, I open a US Weekly magazine and am appeased, elated, and appreciative to see Carmelo Anthony back with his wife La La Anthony, together with their son as a family. I like to think that the experience of Kobe Bryant's death brought the Anthony family back, or closer, together after Carmelo and La La were separated for some time. But also, I like to think the experience brought back together or strengthened marriages, families, friendships and so on all over the world. Life can end too suddenly for us to be at odds with those we truly love, or who truly love us. I am sure many of us have heard this our entire lives. And see, even after death, Kobe is still making us pay close attention while he schools us through the course of his journey. *Show Time* for eternity. A true Los Angeles Laker.

In my Divine mind and spirit the Black Mamba is well and alive. I intuitively and intellectually know that no born soul ever dies. To die means to have never existed to begin with. But instead, each of us as living souls transitions from and through realms of existence elevating until we reach the Almighty Divine conscious state of undisturbed peace. Maturing to reach that stage is what makes us all immortal beyond the flesh. So instead of grieving Kobe, Gianna, and the seven others involved in the crash, or anyone else who has passed on in life, bid them farewell with peace and blessings along their journey to reach eternal lasting peace.

The following is a quote shared from the writings of Florence Scovel Shinn's *Perfect Self-Expression or The Divine Design* I read published in *The Prosperity Bible*:

"…birth and death are man-made laws … the real man, spiritual man, is birthless and deathless! He never was born and has never died—'As he was in the beginning, he is now, and ever shall be!'" Forever live Kobe 'Black Mamba' Bryant.

I, the author Tre Prince, dedicate this passage to all, including the Bryant family: wife Vanessa, and daughters Natalia, Bianka, and Capri. To Kobe's mother, father, and two sisters. And to all his fans. May all live on with peace and blessings.

The Prince

Part 2

~~Creativity~~

The Prince

Chapter 5

Passion.

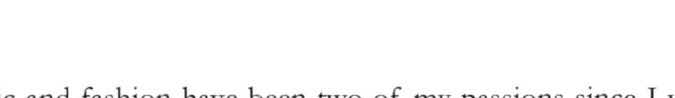

Music and fashion have been two of my passions since I was a pissy little boy. Both are arts of design, and art is naturally a cosmic attraction for me. Colors, drawings, pictures—creativity; orchestrated sound—song, tune, melody, choir, concert, rhythm—creativity; creative ware—design, fabrics, style, coordination—creativity. It is all an attraction to me.

At two years of age, the earliest memory in life I recall, and earliest cosmic attraction, was holding my newly born sister, Chetarah, in my arms and admiring the lime green zip-up onesie pajamas I recall her wearing. Another time, at four years young, it was a mural painting that covered the ceiling and walls of a paternity ward at a hospital where my auntie De De gave birth to my cousin Shanika. I remember being drawn by the artistry of its design and colors.

Growing up as a kid my earliest favorite song (or as it turned out to be) is Shirley Murdock's "As We Lay." My earliest memory of hearing it, I'd just woken from a nap and lay on the living room couch still half asleep. My mother stayed off the corner of 60th and Hyde Park at this time, in a small duplex. I was about three or four years young. But my first impression of the song was that it was a sad song or funeral song that you heard in church. For that reason, in my mind, I associated the song with the meaning of the passing of a life. Which then made it sad, and hearing it played kind of spooked me or gave me goose bumps as a child and early teen. But then I eventually learned the song's words and it turned out that the organ tune, or what sounded to be an organ instrument played in the song, was similar to the sound I would hear in church. Which certainly used to spook me a little as a kid. And my grandmother Mrs. Alice Williams kept me in the church as a child. And so maybe I also attended a funeral at some earlier time, I don't recall, because certainly the organ is played during wakes and funerals. The same organ tune used in scary themed TV shows or movies back then spooked us all as kids. Anyhow, I now love Shirley Murdock's classic "As We Lay." Music has always been an inspiration for me and has given me a passion to compose.

Losing anyone for someone, somewhere, is always hard. Especially when it happens so suddenly. But life is life, according to the way you—we—live life. And so if you readily embrace the happiness of it, then also embrace the sorrow the same. Sorrow isn't necessarily bad; it just means being sad or depressed. But you can be happy-sad or happy-depressed. It is common. Like when losing an elder that passes on after a life fully lived. You're sad or depressed because you'll miss that person. But you feel joy, too that they've gone to a better place. Life goes on regardless of what you think, or how you feel, or however else you respond to it. We are all living in this realm of existence simply for the human experience. And that is exactly what every moment and memory is; an experience of life, lessons, and sometimes sudden changes. By nature or man-made.

COVID-19 is one of those sudden, man-made, and unexpected experiences that brought about sad-depressing sorrow. But again, life, regardless of how you, we, they choose to live it, is about human experiences as it always has been. Live and hate it, or live and love it. That is entirely based on your own perception. If COVID-19 wasn't man-made or didn't paint a terrible tragedy, would the sorrow feel the same: sad-depressing? Or would there be joy under the gray stormy cloud?

Question yourself if you are someone that is finding it hard to rediscover joy again after going through any tough experience. Trust me, you can find joy again. No matter how sad-happy it might feel. The impact a life can have on humanity in a society is beyond, or seems at the moment to be beyond, measure or replacement. For instance, and already stated,

Kobe Bryant and his daughter Gianna, to the Bryant family and beyond. So sorrow can be hard, or take a while to embrace, before we can find joy underneath a grey cloud. But it's there, just as sure as the bright burning sun is still in the sky.

Ellis Marsalis, jazz pianist and educator, dad to fellow musicians Wynton and Branford Marsalis, was a spirit that came into the flesh and taught generations of jazz musicians, including four of his six sons, and recorded fifteen albums. It is quoted, "He was the patriarch of an influential musical family." Still, on April 1, 2020, of this year his soul transcended from this earthly realm of experiences, due to pneumonia brought on by COVID-19, at the sudden and early age of 85. Imagine how the Marsalis family and the music world feels and felt. Beyond measure or replacement. For sad or happy-sorrow. And still, life goes on.

After reading the report of Mr. Ellis Marsalis's passing, I went and further researched his music. I bought several songs, including a couple of his son's music that I like. (By means of a MP3 player I own, and the prison's computer system provided, I am able to do so.) Indeed, this man has made an impact on the culture of music. I can hear his sound playing in many other genres of music than just jazz. I can hear his inspired influence in Grammy award winner John Legend. Who thanked Ellis, I assume, for his contributions to music. I don't recall if the article I read clarified for which reason. However, I now give thanks to Ellis Marsalis for his contributions to the culture of music, "Forever will live your music and teachings."

The Legacy of Sergio Rossi grabs my attention because this was a guy whose footwear was beloved by common folks and celebrities, and the shoe designer world. And simultaneously, I am a fan of footwear. I love a nice pair of shoes, sandals, or boots to compliment the finishing touches of dress. You cannot be sharp in dress if your shoe game is boo boo. A nice clean pair of socks, or bare feet, will go better than a dull or wrong pair of shoes. Trust me.

Anyhow, I never rocked a pair of Rossi's shoes before, but I do dig the Italian designer's craftsmanship. He had style and class. But also the storyline attached to the brand is capturing and inspiring to me. Sergio launched his namesake brand after learning from his father how to make shoes; by 1968 he was already in his thirties. This tells me that he was a man who was still growing and determined in those days. Where many men then, and even now today, reach their thirties and suddenly think they are getting old. Next they suffer from all sorts of mental or physical health conditions, that aren't from natural causes, before they suddenly die before the age of sixty. Women are the same. Someone please stop the madness. It is all a mind thing. This Shit Crazy!

Anyway, Sergio was so determined that he built one of Italy's largest accessory brands. That is pure vision and a manifestation of the mind. I admire the ability and demonstration of it. Then suddenly the Corona virus pandemic swallowed the last days of Sergio Rossi's life. He passed on April 2, 2020, at the bright age of 84. Still his legacy, and his spirit, lives on. And the impact of his contribution to the fashion industry has re-sparked my interest, and I renew my vow to go forward with my own plans and designs I've readied but have set aside for fashion in footwear and clothing. A vision I have had since a late teen, early adult. Thanks Sergio.

In closing, but to a new chapter, may everyone that has been affected by the COVID-19 outbreak now find peace within themselves. Know that your lost ones aren't lost, but instead by divine means have elevated and graduated from this human-earthly experience to the spiritual kingdom of infinite joy and peace. And yeah, I know that it appears for many that lives were shortened or taken too soon, and had it not been for the virus pandemic they all would still be living with us. However true, the reality is that our beloved are gone, and COVID-19 was their exit to the hereafter. An experience we each will share. This Shit Crazy.

Though look at it in a utopian way. Embrace it! Hotep: blessings and peace be to you.

Chapter Six

South Central, The Angels.

Last year (2019) I learned something over again about myself; I truly have no enemies. Absent anger and pain, even with memory, there is no hate I hold towards anyone to consider them as an enemy.

Since the age of eleven I have been considered an active gang member. The summer I graduated elementary school was the same summer I got courted on my set at Manchester Park in my home community. In fact, as I was being initiated I was also initiating my later groove-dog, Chipmunk. He was the same age as me. We both would turn twelve that year, before summer's end. However, by the next summer's end my groove-dog would die by the same gun he lived by. I would watch him try to scramble to his feet after taking a head shot, obviously not aware of his fatal condition. Then within a minute his brain function shut down and he collapsed, lying still.

Instead of the experience withdrawing me from the lifestyle, I sank deeper into it. The only thing to save me from the same fate as Chipmunk's and a lot of others during that era was my closeness to the Spiritual Tree of life; it wasn't my time to go nor was it ever my thought to.

Now, over two decades later I find myself emotionally touched by the death of Nipsy Hussle, who was associated with the Rolling 60s Crips; a rival gang to my association with the Infinite West Side Hoova Crips and Criminals. Since a teenager I had been gangbanging against the 60s and all relative Owes or Neighborhood Crips, and other labeled 'enemy' sets in the streets of LA. Not just in the streets but also in juvenile hall, camp, CYA, and when locked up in the LA County Jail.

But then I noticed as I scaled the levels of incarceration that gangbanging ceased to exist to a great extent once I hit the California State Penitentiary system, the CDC (Ironwood). Where reputable OGs from all sides, Crips, Bloods, Seranos, weren't having it for the most part, and instead gave a young active gangbanger some Black, Brown, or Spiritual literature to sit down and read and hoped that it would change at least one mind before it was too late. The same is true even more so here in the feds on the yard. Made me sit down both then, and now later, and consciously question how come this same structure isn't out in the streets where it needs to count the most. Because what sense is it to get locked up, especially if for gang related crimes, and against rivals who you're now doing time with, and everyone for the most part that is around you has the same desire to get back to the streets or to their family? Not to repeat the cycle over again—and that's if you are blessed to see the streets again.

When a man starts asking himself these types of conscious questions, and answering them, that is when he is starting to think. And think outside the box!

But unfortunately, the reality for many, including myself once upon a time, happens to be to repeat the cycle over and over again. Why? Because you're not thinking, nor thinking outside the box. Or not strong enough yet to follow your self outside the box. This doesn't only apply to gang or street culture. This applies to all of life in general, when facing detrimental obstacles that keep recurring based on your poor, repetitive actions. Poor judgment. Poor decision making… I ponder whether the dead, if they could waken from the grave to relive again, as if paroled from prison, sadly too would repeat the same cycle that led to their death? Possibly so. This Shit Crazy!

As an individual I stood and looked at myself in the mirror. I had to. I am fed up with not thinking, or thinking outside the box, or not following my self outside the box. And what I seen in the mirror, and still see today, is a lok—no doubt! But not just any l'ok; I am THA Intellectual L'OK. This is where the difference is drawn and educated thinking, gang members, street dudes, or whatever we've been called or call ourselves, reach common ground with the best of thinkers by means of common sense. We are no different than the average politicians on Capitol Hill, blue collar businessmen on Wall Street, high ranking service officials in the military, or working class citizens when using our minds for greatness and a greater cause. And so I create and use the terminology, intellectual lok or loc, intellectual gangsta, intellectual thug, because I am speaking and making reference directly to those of us who've been misunderstood by society and deemed a menace. And also I personally address those of us who've been labeled as gangbangers, gang members, gangstas, children of the ghetto, the underprivileged, minorities—yet we are intelligent, talented, and educated. That it is past due for us as individuals, and then our hoods as a whole, to step our matha fuck'n bang up and get cracc'n and popp'n in these streets on all intellectual levels! No more gaining to lose or getting out of prison to then try to gain back again. But instead now, gain to retain! Homes, schools, businesses—our communities—our lives!

What Nipsey Hussle proved, as did many in the streets of LA before his time and now even still, is that the extent of the effect our social-environment condition has on us is optional. Remember, and as I mentioned in an earlier chapter was quoted to me by my homeboy, "We are only limited by the restrictions we place on ourselves in the end." Just because you are born in poverty doesn't make you impoverished, but for what you allow yourself to think and believe. The same if you were born in the hood; it doesn't mean that you have to gangbang or if you gangbang then that's all you can be. What? Never!

This brotha Nipsey, intellectual loc, looked around the box that he was created in, saw what he could use or make of his predicament with his talent and intelligence, and stepped outside the box to flourish in prosperity. And he was prolific. The only sad thing about it is that the conditions of the box he stepped from, but doubled back to rebuild, would bring about the demise of his efforts in achievement, of the further distance he could have excelled outside the box. And brought back even greater tools to rebuild with. However, he still excelled regardless, and left behind a legacy that has been impactful.

I myself have been inspired by the achievements of this more-than-gang-member. Which now further influences me to be more than a gang member, or anything else classified from within the box I too was created in. And I also follow in the footsteps or follow the train of thought of the many, to obtain greater tools to rebuild the box. Or better yet, demolish it.

At first I was slightly biased toward Nipsey's music because of my mindset at the time and our opposite gang affiliation. However, I have always acknowledged his talent as a rapper/MC. But then I started paying attention to his moves as a businessman and thinker. Dropping a mix tape and retailing it at $100; what noncommercial local rapper does that? Then Jay-Z buys a thousand copies. Major. Then I later hear that he impeded demolition of the roller skating rink World On Wheels, keeping it from being eradicated from LA's urban culture. And then purchasing it to maintain its existence. That was a respectable move between him and rapper YG. That roller skating rink is our history. At least thirty-five years of generations. I started going there at the age of six and I believe my mother threw me a birthday party there around the same age if I recall correctly. Anyhow, many memories, is the point I make. The place is a landmark.

Next, the man commercializes the street corners of Slauson and Crenshaw, giving it more buzz than it ever had, before capitalizing on his promotion by opening the Marathon Clothing Store on now prime commercial real estate. That was smooth. By the time he dropped his first debut album *Victory Lap* in 2018, I was all in, like his record label (which I learned of after his death) with banging his music.

I recall Nipsey before he was Nipsey, though without personally knowing him, back when he was a young boy. His family were the only foreign-looking Africans that stood outside the entrance/exit parking lot of the Slauson Swap Meet selling incense and so on in the late 1990s and early 2000s. When he started putting out mix tapes, and I inquired where he'd sprung up from, talking like a certified reputable from the 60s, I felt I should have known or heard of him prior. But I hadn't. In reply I kept being told to remember the African family that used to be outside the Slauson Swap Meet selling incense. And that he was the little boy of the family.

I was with an older homeboy of mine once who bought a pack of incense from Nipsey and his father; another time a homeboy and I tried hollering at his sister—I assume she was—but who was too disciplined to do anything but blush with her father close by; and the last time I recall

I saw him, me and others, again were coming out of the Slauson Swap Meet in early 2000 and bumped into him and his older brother, Blacc, who sold CDs. Funny, you just never know who you might cross paths with, never speak to or acknowledge or remember, yet that person later becomes someone significant in society. Or who impacts your life.

CHAPTER 7

A MAN FALLS, HIS LEGACY RISES.

When rumor first began spreading that Nipsey Hussle had been shot and killed, I hadn't been gone from USP-Atwater but for two months. I'd only been here at AUSP-Thomson a couple weeks over thirty days. And so it was word of mouth at first, until I called to the streets, then afterwards newspaper and magazines began publishing the story. But before the confirmation that it was his own home boy that pulled the trigger, I absolutely thought it was gang related. I had been hearing for years how he was known to be seen out on Slauson and Crenshaw at times, then later at times in front of his clothing store. So when it was reported that the killing had happened in front of his store, I definitely assumed that he had got caught slipping by a rival in feud with the Rolling 60s.

However, I did not feel elated or indifferent about the incident. Instead, the news hit me as though I intimately knew Nipsey, or he was a member of my community. Strangely so. But it's the truth. I later expressed this same truth over the phone when I called to the streets and spoke with my cousin Baycee from 74 Hoova that was standing somewhere present with a member of the 83 Gangsta Crips. This was within the first week of the incident occurring. And I was then informed that the slaying was an in-house beef and not gang related.

I felt somewhat relieved knowing now that there wouldn't be a retaliation feud in the streets that for sure could cause more deaths. When a small grace period the streets in South Central LA had been quiet and peaceful for a couple months. At least on my side of town, that is.

But anyhow, I expressed too over the phone that the little dude's death (Nipsey Hussle) shouldn't have been, because of the envelope he was pushing for black business ownership in the hood, and him helping raise the census level of consciousness in the streets. That's what affected me the most. An intellectual loc had been lost and by someone that can't replace him. Regardless of what set he banged. And my point there was felt before I hung up the phone.

It hit even harder later when after his death I learned of the further accomplishments and contributions Nipsey had made and achieved: a co-working space and STEM center in his neighborhood called Vector 90, Destination Crenshaw—an open air museum devoted to celebrating the achievements of Black artists—his independent record label All In No Money Out, teamed up with Atlantic Records. Plus he owned a barber shop and fish market in the same strip mall he'd helped drop millions of dollars on to own the plaza in efforts to buy back the block and provide a location for other and future Black-owned businesses to thrive.

Overall he was for the raising up rather than the demise of our people and community. That is the exact mentality of an intellectual gangbanger or member. Yeah we might bang the set or bang on you because that is what most of us grew up doing as a product of our environment. And likely we will die in our environment, as it turned out to be for Nipsey. A common thing. Still, it doesn't ceter one's love, leadership, or dedication to one's community and its body of people. It is an obligation desired and embraced with open arms, and always will be until after the day we overcome this mental sickness of ours.

In furtherance of this LA West Coast mentality I have briefly laid out here, Nipsey himself stated, "I understand my obligation. I got an obligation to my community first, my family first, to hoods like LA all around the country, who live for the culture." (Documented from columnists Anika Reed and Rasha Ali.)

It is how I and all intellectual gangbangers and members feel and think. We are the revolutionaries, educators, great leaders and greater followers, activists, and philanthropists of our race, people, gangs, and community. Without us there is no hope, faith, direction, or positive examples for those who are born into this cycle. Or that are attracted to the struggle-street-gang lifestyle and culture.

But not only are intellectual gangbangers or members effective and productive in this regard within our communities and amongst our race of people, but also so is any intellectual man or woman that comes from or understands the same plight as we do. It is why lives of this magnitude (2Pac, Malcom X, Nipsey Hussle, George and Johnathan Jackson, Fred Hampton, Marcus Garvey, Fidel Castro, Nat Turner, Assata Shakur, and more) have had such an impact on history and in our society.

Each one, when taking on their roles in life, knew what time it was before they filled the shoes each was to individually walk in. No different than how I know myself what time it is, for penning this memoir, and when I step free. On Hoova!

"That's a part of the game, the way I see it. I have a duty to justify the seat that I'm sitting in. Nobody has any success on his own."—Nipsey Hussle.

Chapter 8

Motivation

I stand behind the words of Nipsey Hussle when he wrote in *The Player's Tribune* in 2018: "I have a duty to justify the seat that I'm sitting in. Nobody has any success on his own." This is a moral principle instilled in you as an adolescent or tiny homey when growing up and being trained and molded in the streets of LA, or within its gang culture. He learned it, I and others learned it, and it was being taught well before we came along. And it is still a moral reminder today, as long as we live, and anyone who holds any position or royalties lives.

You touch a bag, you break bread; you receive or see the vision, you share it; you take the driver's seat, you have the responsibility to get us to our destination. Love, loyalty, and honor is the cause and effect for each of these acts of principle that are so very much valued. By all that agree.

For many, we grew up living to embrace the moment of position, providing or spreading royalties. It is a form of G status because it represents leadership and camaraderie, or having a voice or a duty amongst comrades; recognition for the sacrifice of putting it all on the line, especially for the greatest causes. This act is the spirit in men you cannot buy with money or have melted and poured on you. It comes born from the Infinite Source that is within you. Either you believe it, or you don't. But if you do then it doesn't matter what the risks are along the journey, as long as the goal and outcome supports the objective in the end. For Nipsey, as for many, it was to finish the marathon.

The marathon—1: a long distance race especially on foot. 2: an endurance contest—has been the conquest for Africans in the Americas, the Islands, and on other lands of the Western World since our fall from God's or Allah's grace and our later enslavement. To return to that heaven experience on earth is the goal.

But what we all must understand is that this long distance race is not and has never been a physical race in any aspect of pursuing it. Instead, it is a spiritual marathon in every facet of its conquest. To return to a 'heaven state of mind': in all prior years the contest of endurance has been one of pain and suffering, because as a people we have been turned away from our souls and their spiritual tools of energy, which are the source of receiving all things created, in each of us, in the likeness of God.

But we have been tricked and made to live outwardly and the furthest from our souls now for over four hundred years. And doing so is the root cause of our ignorance, suffering, and enslavement.

Listen! There has never been a whip cracked on any man or woman's soul, regardless of race or creed. Nor a chain or shackle placed on the soul. Or a soul placed in prison, a concentration camp, or gas chamber. That is all told to trick you and keep you living outwardly, attached to the physical world and your physical body as God's Kingdom or the devil's hell. Folly.

We cannot complete or excel past the marathon by running it physically. It has to be accomplished spiritually because we are all spiritual beings. To simply do this you have to use the mind—it is the great tool of the soul. The world is nothing more than a physical experience, for each of our creation of it and in it. The Master of Deception knows this and uses it to conquer and control.

Nipsey Hussle picked up the torch and was continuing the marathon of Jesus Christ—Yehoshua started the race and endurance contest long ago when he sacrificed his God-given human experience to prove to us that it isn't about the physical life we live but the spiritual. Our sins committed are against each of our individual souls spiritually. You are spiritually saved simply when you start thinking godly and then turn inwardly from the "physical world" of sin.

All those I previously mentioned that have impacted history and our society have run this marathon. But also included are Harriet Tubman, who ran her part; Hazrat Inayat Khan, Marcus Gravey, Martin Luther King Jr., Elijah Muhammod, Louis Farrahkhan, Mahatma Gandhi, Che Guevara, and so forth have all run the course. Any man, woman, child, or beast who has come in the flesh and while living gave guidance, made or was made a sacrifice to awaken the people from within have run the marathon or is still running it today: you and I.

One day I would like to meet Nipsey Hussle's mother. She is a spiritual being and blessing here in the flesh to help show those who choose to learn the way to heaven and peace on earth within our own individual selves. I listened to the speech she gave at the 2019 BET Awards during the segment dedicated to her son. She was the strongest spirit I'd heard in a long time outside of my own. The comfort and peace in her voice, mind, and soul was powerful. That night I felt reassured that God is alive in the flesh. And all anyone else has to do to know the same is turn inward and witness the phenomenon that is truly a spiritual reality. She held no pain or sorrow but instead joy and peace for her son. While most, if not all, around her grieved with tears and pain for the life she carried, bore, and gave birth to. That is powerful.

I did not see Nipsey's mother visually in physical form because I followed the show by listening to it on my MP3 player. Because I could not view the TV from the cell that I was in. However, I heard my primitive ancestors when I heard Nipsey's mother's soul speak. That experience was powerful. And if you listened to her but didn't hear what I heard or greater—That Shit Crazy!

Wake up people! This is a great parable you are missing.

Chapter 9

Closer

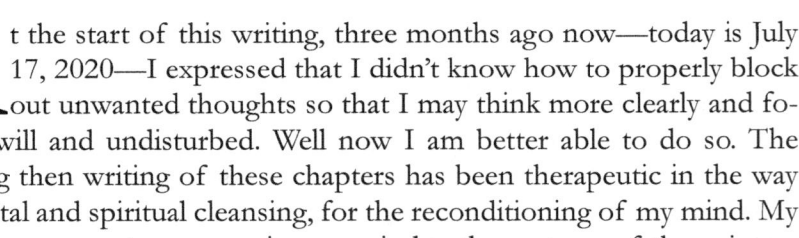

At the start of this writing, three months ago now—today is July 17, 2020—I expressed that I didn't know how to properly block out unwanted thoughts so that I may think more clearly and focus at will and undisturbed. Well now I am better able to do so. The thinking then writing of these chapters has been therapeutic in the way of mental and spiritual cleansing, for the reconditioning of my mind. My Soul. In response to me opening my mind to the vastness of the universe and allowing the Infinite Spirit within me to flow freely, I received by law of attraction spiritual instruction from my Superconscious mind: the Universal Mind, how to construct my conscious and subconscious mind. Now I too build my kingdom to come on earth as it is in heaven—within. And readily it is, Truth Made Manifested, through Christ within me.

Remember I stated back in the introduction how I followed criminal case law like how the disciples followed Jesus Christ seeking instruction and blessing from the Father Yahweh in heaven, hoping to receive a favorable outcome in my case on appeal? Well, that form of thought and belief is equivalent to putting my trust in man; a sinful error on my behalf. But it turns out to have been a blessing that I awakened from such a dormant way of thinking and enslavement to my own self. The only law I am to put my trust in is Divine Spiritual Law: the natural law of the Universe, the highest law of creation and governed by the Almighty Creator within me. In essence I am the same in metaphor as Jesus Christ: Truth Made Manifest. This has been my transformational creed by the Infinite Spirit of Ausar. Or else what would I, a child born in the ghetto, of Jehovah's Creed, be, if not 'I AM HE Who Created Me to BE!'

Man's law: criminal law or civil, is straight up and down bullshit: devil's law. Trickery disguised in the form of arguments of interpretation designed for gamesmanship. It is why two lawyers or judges can argue what is supposed to be a single truth in separate ways that are opposed to the other's. They even call the other's truth a lie but use the jargon, wrong interpretation of the law or misapplication of the law and so on, all while under sworn solemn oath. And who is right? Well by traditional Greek custom, whoever's argument is best persuasive... Know the Captor. This Shit Crazy!

Quickly, as a prime example of man's law. The case I mentioned earlier, US v. Ray Chea, where the district judge that presided in that case ruled that the crime of Hobbs's Act Robbery is not a "crime of violence" by definition because it can be committed without causing physical harm but instead by threat of future injury to property. Remember? Well, here you have it several months later after that ruling, the Ninth Circuit Court of Appeals makes an imposing ruling in US v. Dominguez that a Hobbs Act Robbery is a "crime of violence." Supporting its findings and ruling by a different interpretation of the same criminal statues and judgement cases that the district court used to say that it is not!

So then the question is: how in the fuck can the interpretation be anything than what is or should be clear cut? Simple. Because it is devil's law to begin with. Which is the judicial foundation of America's Constitution. The same constitution that obliterated the Natives in America of their land, freedom, and culture. And eradicated some tribes from history. Know the Captor (cause) and free yourself from being its captive (the effect).

I have said to myself and to others now for thirteen years or more that I genuinely embrace and, in a sense, appreciate the experience of my incarceration. I wouldn't have asked for it, but I accept it nonetheless. Why? Because even when I couldn't see it quite clearly at first I've seen enough to know that there was light at the end of the tunnel. Not physical light, but light that manifests Truth. That awakens the Soul or helps it redeem the light of God that is within. Just knowing that gave me the sense that I was being preserved and prepared for something Divine, more than the sensory pleasures or anger I had entertained destructively at the start of this journey.

After being convicted, again after my direct appeal was denied, and even last year in April or May when my 2255 habeas corpus petition for relief was shot down, I felt reason to say F the world. But I didn't have divine right to do so. Although frustrated, that wasn't cause to say F it all. Besides, that is not how Divine Law or divine energy works. What is Divine is pure and untainted by emotions or worldly affairs that are dying. Therefore I knew anger, stress, or violence wouldn't help bring about the change I desired. But instead, proper prayer, faith, and discipline would: 'Seek and ye shall find,' 'Knock and ye shall be answered,' 'Ask and ye shall receive.'

Throughout this journey of sixteen years, I have gone through phases of believing in God to questioning whether God truly exists; from believing I was God, without there being a Superior entity than me, to believing I am nothing without a Superior entity than me; then at last, coming to the realization that I and the Creator am one and the same. As the Son, the Father, and Holy Spirit are all one Divine entity. But I had to see it through to get to this stage in life. 'Wisdom has always foretold that one must see the cause through to its end so as to understand Allah's test and what HE has in reward for you.' This I find is the desired effect, by Divine Cause, from my incarceration. That is my faith.

Five years ago I started entertaining the thought of me and Nipsey Hussle meeting and sitting down at some point after I am released, and together as intellectuals and businessmen, coming up with even greater solutions to bring forth prosperity in health, wealth, and education within our respective communities, in addition to his existing accomplishments. But first, I had to sit down with respected intellectual gang members from various hoods in LA to establish peace and order. That critical piece has to be the foundation for real change to exist in the streets of LA. Anyhow, I still after his passing hold this thought and vision that whoever is heir to his estate is also heir to carrying out his unfinished plans coherent with his overall mentality. And that we can work together in honor of Nipsey and others. Because as it is being understood throughout the nation, 'The Marathon still continues.' And I'm coming home with my spiritual running shoes on and laced up.

I would someday like to meet Kobe and Gigi Bryant's family out of homage and respect to Kobe. As well as collaborate with Vanessa Bryant on the children's book project the Black Mamba created. And to help broaden awareness of Kobe's foundation, which gave back to the community but that neither I personally, nor anyone I know in my community, had known anything about until after his death. That should not have been so. Not when the communities of South Central, Watts, Compton, Long Beach, Inglewood, West LA, Carson, San Pedro, Pasadena, Lynwood, on out to Pamona, Riverside, and San Bernardino all honored and respected the Black Mamba. Forever may his legacy live on.

Tonight I ride out to the piano keys of Ellis Marsalis and let the symphony of jazz carry me into the right and to wherever I arrive in thought … COVID-19 has made a resurgence after showing signs of possibly being contained; at least enough to where most of the country had begun opening up after months of lock-down then modified operations. Similar to here in prison. But now the country has a new problem that is just as disruptive as COVID-19; it has been dealing with it since after I began this memoir. The killing of George Floyd, an unarmed Black man by police in Minneapolis, Minnesota. This occurred shortly after the killing of an innocent Black woman, Breonna Taylor, by police in Kentucky. Both incidents and others, all coupled together, have incited a massive riot and protest throughout the nation in many cities that is still carrying on over a month later. And in the State of Oregon a protest group has taken up a section of a community it has deemed sovereign from state and federal officials intervening. Maybe not the best thought out plan, but certainly intellectual thinking. American society within a span of four months has gone from a state of pandemic and banding together in symphony and harmony to pull through the crisis, to now a state of civil unrest and violence.

And the latest frenzy is that Kanye West has entered the race for the presidential election, as he promised he would years ago. That's what's up; President West in 2020. It makes a good inspiration for others if nothing more. Besides, the radical left wing is trying their damnedest to eject President Donald Trump from the White House so that their own party can move in. Even at the cost of failing the economy, stirring up violent protests and rioters, and reporting manipulative reports concerning the statistics of COVID-19. All in the scheme of politics. But what is most disturbing to me is how easily influenced a mind that is not self-controlled is. All the people that are mentally wrapped up in the madness that is going on. This is a cause for urgency in spiritual guidance.

Clearly the Democrats or the Republicans aren't dishing out spiritual guidance. Both have their personal and hidden immoral agendas. If neither hadn't, and their intentions were pure, then they would have come together and worked hand in hand to destroy the coronavirus before it rose to the stage of a pandemic. Or surely after it had. But they didn't and still haven't, thoroughly. And there would not be or have been a massive nation-wide riot and protest even in the wake of George and Breonna's deaths had the parties acted effectively and in unity.

Instead, each party stands at odds with the other for political power. Smearing and defaming each other's name and character, ignorantly. It is sad to see the party leaders of a country act out in such behavior as though they were cast members of a drama-driven reality TV show. It is nearly like tuning into *Love-N-Hip-Hop*, *Jersey Shore*, *Mob Wives*, or any other brain dead entertainment. Just with the addition of global politics as the primary narrative or theme.

But again, what is disturbing is the minds of all the people that tune in to get their dose of destructive thinking: the effect of a lack of Divine Knowledge, light, and good to cancel out ignorance, blindness, and evil. Which equals to a mind-spirit that is not self-controlled.

I pray (command, demand, praise, thanksgiving) that the Infinite Spirit in all its purity and power that is omnipotent, omniscience, omnipresent by thought and in all that is created, is learned of by the masses then used to recondition their minds, that then will recondition the way we all live. Everything that is happening in this country today and throughout many other parts of the world is the result from the way we've been conditioned to think: in constant fear, anxiety, anger, hate, envy, poverty, and overall ignorance. This discordance affects the harmonious nature of our entire divine being. But it is curable. To help bring peace, equilibrium and plainly a better way of life in the world, we simply must recondition our thoughts.

For instance. By travel and or research, look at the places of the world that are inhabited by indigenous people. Many, if not all, are not going through what we here are going through in the modern world. They don't even have a clue about COVID-19, cops killing Blacks, racial injustice, protests, or riots. Instead, most, if not all, are in a state of peace. Simply because they are at peace in their minds, which further makes them in complete harmony with the earth's and universe's natural laws governed through the Infinite Spirit which is the source of all natural thought—cause and effect. Omnipotent, omniscience, and omnipresent. And what is natural is purity and peace.

Not only can you look at indigenous people who distance themselves from the modern world, but there are people here living in our modern society that are not affected by what is going on. And never will be. How come? Simply because of how they have conditioned their minds to a natural state of peace. And so from that natural state they see the world or this society as being in it, but not of it. That train of thought will protect anyone from being gravely affected by what is going on around them. Let's all learn to protect our minds the same. Amen.

Last, this is not the end. This memoir is only but the first chapter of the biography to come. Today I am great; tomorrow I will be greater. My greatness has yet to be lived. For now, Hotepu.

Read other Titles by Tre Prince

Bounce Back Joe

My Spiritual Redemption

On My Way Back To The Hereafter

Back From The Hereafter

Stanky Banky

www.ingramcontent.com/pod-product-compliance
Lightning Source LLC
Chambersburg PA
CBHW071914070526
44583CB00016B/1986